P9-DMO-152

Jeannette Rankin

The Lady from Montana.

The New York Public Library

JEANNETTE RANKIN

FIRST LADY IN CONGRESS

A Biography

HANNAH JOSEPHSON

The Bobbs-Merrill Company, Inc.
INDIANAPOLIS NEW YORK

Published by the Bobbs-Merrill Company, Inc.
Indianapolis New York

ISBN 0-672-51921-6
Library of Congress catalog card number 74-3887
Designed by Ingrid Beckman
Manufactured in the United States of America

Second printing

For my sisters, old friends and allies

Contents

Prologue

The debate in the House of Representatives on the declaration of war against Japan after the attack on Pearl Harbor on December 7, 1941 lasted only forty minutes, so great was the consensus of the members. Only one voice was raised against the war resolution: that of Miss Jeannette Rankin of Montana. Amid the clamor she rose again and again to speak, only to be shouted down by her colleagues and ignored by the Speaker. When the roll call came she was at last heard: "As a woman I can't go to war, and I refuse to send anyone else." Her "Nay" drew forth a chorus of boos and catcalls from the floor and the galleries, later to be echoed by denunciations from press and pulpit all over the country.

Jeannette Rankin was not surprised by this reaction; it was almost incredibly a repeat of a scene in which she had figured before, in the very same place. Some twenty years earlier she had come to Washington as the first woman elected to Congress, just as the United States was about to plunge into World War I. In April 1917 her personal dilemma was far more difficult to resolve than in 1941, for she was untried as a legislator, and the eyes of the world were upon her. When she made her first appearance in the House of Representatives it was common knowledge that President Woodrow Wilson would call on the Congress to declare war against Germany. (That was the way it was done in those days, and in 1941 as well.) The pressure on Miss Rankin to vote in favor of the war resolution was prodigious and came from all sides, from fellow suffragists, from some of her best friends, from political allies, and particularly from the brother to whom she was so deeply attached. It was her brother Wellington who pleaded with her, ironically, as it seems now, to vote "a man's vote." How could she vote a man's vote? She was a woman. A man's vote would be a vote for "lawful" killing, and as a woman she could only cast her vote for life.

During the debate in the House on the war resolution in 1917, she sat mute through many hours of fervid oratory, weeping unashamedly from time to time, but when she responded to the roll call—having exhausted her tears, as she said later—she arose dry-eyed to make a simple statement: "I love my country, but I cannot vote for war."

Her record is thus unique: the only member of Congress who voted against United States involvement in two world wars. But if that were all there was to distinguish her from others, she would rate no more than a footnote in history as an impractical idealist cast in the wrong role. She was more than that; she was a dynamic figure in the true American tradition, and in the course of a long and fruitful life she became a symbol to great numbers of people, as a suffragist and feminist, as a pacifist, as a political reformer, and as an example of how life could be maintained to a great age with meaning and purpose.

Although she held office for only two terms in Congress, the second more than twenty years after the first, for most of her life politics was her medium and her chosen arena; she lived and breathed politics, which she saw as the principal avenue to needed social change. The art of politics, the design of government, and especially the legislative process absorbed her, while the practical shifts necessary for their conduct never brought disillusionment.

It is one of the anomalies of American life that a politician of such benign character should have emerged from Montana, whose local government, under the sway of the Anaconda Copper Company, made the depredations of the Tweed Ring in New York seem the work of rank amateurs. Miss Rankin entered politics through the suffrage movement, which tapped a vein of potential voters not yet under the domination of "The Company." She led the women of Montana to win the vote, and having once tasted victory in that area, she never lost her appetite for it. When she was ninety years old she said: "I never left Congress. I was there with Wayne Morse and Ernest Gruening, voting against the Tonkin Bay Resolution."

Both in and out of Congress she conducted herself like a professional politician, even though the issues she adopted were ignored by most professionals. She not only fought for women's rights to vote and hold office; she advanced other measures to do away with sexual discrimination; she took her stand against economic injustice and in favor of civil rights. Believing that wars were not only evil but futile, she devoted herself between two world wars to tireless lobbying for antiwar legislation. And for the last twenty years of her life, convinced that outworn electoral procedures thwarted the democratic process, she agitated in favor of new methods to make them more responsive to the needs and will of the people. Fiorello LaGuardia said of her: "This woman has more courage and packs a harder punch than a regiment of regular-line politicians."

Her career has further significance: she was an active agitator, a "good agitator," in Emerson's words, for more than six decades, right up to her death as she approached the age of ninety-three. Young people were drawn to her as one who shared their resentments and their aspirations; to those of an older generation who look to their last years with dread, as a period of withdrawal and desuetude, she proved that no one need fear that time of life who goes on "pursuing ends that give our existence a meaning," as Simone de Beauvoir has written.

It was my good fortune to meet Miss Rankin in 1950 and to know her during the last twenty years of her life, thanks to our mutual friend Katharine Anthony, with whom she stayed whenever she came to New York. I was captivated by her instant friendliness, her way of reaching out to people and making their concerns hers, which went far to explain her success with voters. It was not an act; it was instinctive with her, as I had occasion to observe. She was still sprightly at seventy, with a low-pitched, musical voice and a ready smile, feminine in an old-fashioned manner, aiming to please. But longer acquaintance gave me more insights into her character. I learned that she was tough-minded, tenacious in argument, impatient with triflers. Her artless exterior concealed a woman of intense feelings and powerful convictions.

We had many meetings during the writing of this book, in the course of which she answered all my queries with the utmost candor, showing an astonishing memory for important events long past, along with touches that gave them immediacy. I was her guest in Georgia and, toward the end of her life, in California, where in spite of her frailty she evinced the same unflagging spirit that had dominated her career.

That career was directed toward an ideal: the ideal of a world at peace, ruled by democratic principles, with equality for all. A large order, yet she was fully aware that it was not to be realized within her lifetime. "You take people as far as they will go," she used to say, "not as far as you would like them to go." But she never stopped trying to set them on the right path. Toward the end of her life William Fitts Ryan summed up her long struggle when he thanked her for coming before a congressional committee and "getting us to think about the unthinkable."

Jeannette Rankin

I

Montana Girlhood

To be a child in Montana in the 1880s was to know mountains and rivers and plains and a great sky overhead enclosing and projecting your world; to live among settlers, miners, ranchers and cowboys; to see Indians riding by to new hunting grounds or decked out for ritual dances; to come upon deer, elk, porcupine or an occasional bear without surprise; to watch the empty countryside filling up and towns spreading out around you. Jeannette Rankin was a child in Montana in those days.

It was a colorful period, encapsulating the exploitation of the continent in a brief span of years, offering adventure, danger, and the promise of untold riches to those hardy souls willing to undertake the risks and endure the fatigues of pioneering, a promise not always fulfilled but granting an optimism and a readiness for innovation, both social and political, to all who lived through it. On settling in the empty American West, it has often been observed, men and women saw the range of the possible extended far beyond what had been imagined in the stratified societies of Europe or the more populous areas of the eastern seaboard and the Middle West. Along with a larger area of freedom, they acquired a greater sense of equality because of struggles shared and difficulties overcome. It is true that the equality they cherished was to some degree based on the exclusion of the Indians whom they had expropriated, just as the equality of white southerners rested on the slavery and oppression of the blacks. But women were from the first accorded almost equal rank with men because of their acknowledged role in the rigors of settlement, although years were to pass before the legal restrictions on their political and property rights were removed.

Jeannette Rankin was born in 1880, nine years before the Montana Territory was admitted to statehood, and in the course of her life witnessed the development of that virgin land into one of the great copper-producing and cattle-raising areas of the country. During the swift transformation pioneer farmers were replaced by ranchers with vast domains, and venturesome gold miners gave way to giant corporations employing thousands of workers to dig that far more serviceable metal, copper, out of the mountains. As Montana grew to figure in the affairs of the nation and the world, so did Jeannette's horizons expand, until they came to encompass the deepest concerns of human beings everywhere.

The child Jeannette was lucky in her parents. Her father, John Rankin, was one of nine children of Scottish immigrants who had settled on a farm in Ontario, Canada, in the early years of the nineteenth century. The farm offered only a meager livelihood for a large family, and John had little schooling, although he learned the carpenter's trade before he was twenty. In 1869 he and his brother Duncan, lured by tales of a gold strike in the Montana Territory, decided to go there in search of fortune. John found his fortune not in gold but in his chest of carpenter's tools, which he loaded onto a small boat on the Missouri River. The boat went aground on a sand bar forty miles from Fort Benton and had to be abandoned, but the tool chest was saved. As he told his children, he carried the chest on his back a long distance before he contrived a handcart to transport it. The worst of the long trek to Fort Benton, then an important supply and transfer point, was the lack of water, for in order to gain time he kept to the high banks above the river, descending to the valley only when driven by thirst.

After a brief stay in Fort Benton, where he bought a team of oxen, he went on to Helena in a fruitless search for work, and thence to Unionville, remaining there for a season to build a stamp mill for crushing ore. He had a fling at prospecting for gold near Cedar Creek, then in 1870 proceeded to Missoula, a village on the banks of the river of that name, and settled in as a builder and contractor. His brother Duncan soon joined him there.

The Missoula River, otherwise known as the Clark Fork, is a branch of the Columbia River, on the Pacific slope of the Continental Divide. Missoula itself is at a comparatively low altitude —3,223 feet—with a mild climate and generous rainfall; the valley in which it is situated is the best fruit-growing area in all Montana. Between the mountain ranges enclosing the valley are rich fields suitable for the raising of a variety of agricultural products.

As the village grew into a town of some importance, John Rankin played an active part in its development: he built the first bridge to span the river, a wooden structure in two sections, taking advantage of an island in the middle of the stream; he also built a church, shops, and dwellings for the new settlers who kept arriving in a steady flow, becoming in the process one of the eminent citizens of the community. Within a few years he was prosperous enough to buy a ranch about six miles from Missoula, within sight of the Bitter Root Mountains.

Among the new arrivals in town was Olive Pickering, a small, lively, competent girl from New Hampshire, who came to Missoula in 1878 under the protection of her uncle, C. W. Berry, one of the founding fathers. Miss Pickering, the second schoolteacher in the territory, held her classes in a one-room building surrounded by a fence on which it was not unusual to see a group of Indians perched, listening impassively to the lessons being chanted within. (One wonders whether they suspected that religious rites were being carried on inside the little shack.) Before a year had elapsed, however, the town lost Miss Pickering's services, for in 1879 she was married to John Rankin, and the following year she gave birth to a daughter, Jeannette, the first of a brood of seven, of whom six survived.

Jeannette was born in the ranchhouse on June 11, 1880. The winter that followed was one of the hardest the settlers had known, and although the heavy snow, as the old records put it, "nourished an especially good grass crop," John Rankin decided that it might not nourish an especially good crop of children.

The Rankin home in Missoula, about 1889, before the trees around it grew tall. On the roof below the cupola are Jeannette, on the left, and Wellington, on the right.

When Jeannette was about five years old, therefore, the growing family moved into town to a house he had built for them. It was at 134 Madison Street, on the very site where Meriwether Lewis, the explorer, had camped on his return from the Pacific in 1806. The house was the most imposing residential building in Missoula, with a first floor finished in red brick, the second floor faced with shingles somewhat in the mansard style, and the whole crowned by a square cupola with a hip roof. There were two small porches in front and a long side porch later to be screened in and used for sleeping in the summer. To remind his wife of her New England surroundings John Rankin planted a lilac bush and a row of elm trees that grew to enormous size. Two pines flanking the gate, apple trees in the yard, and a Virginia creeper over the sleeping porch flourished in that benign climate. Eclectic though it was in style, the house had dignity and charm, not to speak of the latest "modern conveniences," such as central hot-air heating, hot and cold running water, and a bathroom equipped with a tin tub—the first in Missoula to boast of these amenities. From the yard and from the north windows one could see Missoula's outstanding landmark, the mountain called Jumbo, whose treeless elephantine form loomed up from several miles away, dominating the valley.

Until she was in her twenties Jeannette spent her winters in the house in Missoula and her summers at the ranch. The ranch was more like a New England farm than a Western ranch of today; here John Rankin added to his income as a building contractor by raising hay and grain and a few head of cattle, selling milk and butter, and marketing apples from a sizable orchard. A large stand of wood on the property also enabled him to conduct a thriving lumber business, logging in winter and running a sawmill in the summer, thus providing the raw material for his own enterprises as well as for sale to others.

Despite the elegance of the town house and the eminence of their parents in town affairs, the Rankin children were deeply attached to the ranch, where life was larger, more free, richer in excitement. The family had grown at regular intervals; after Jeannette came Philena (who died at an early age), then Harriet, Wellington, Mary, Grace and Edna. As the only boy, Wellington (named after a doctor who had once saved John Rankin's life, not after the Iron Duke) received special treatment, but if anyone was the leader of the children, it was probably Jeannette. As the eldest she was kept busy helping her mother look after the younger ones, along with other household chores such as housecleaning, bedmaking and canning. Wellington remembered that she often read to them in the evenings, and that her eyes would be filled with tears when she read certain Bible stories. She had no duties in connection with the farm, although her sharp powers of observation made her familiar with all its aspects. John Rankin, well acquainted with the daily tyranny of farm work since his boyhood, would not allow his girls to learn to milk a cow, because, he said, "if you know how to do it, there will come times when you'll *have* to do it." It was not impossible in those days to get hired hands to do the farm chores.

They were a close-knit family, affectionate yet highly individualistic. The parents expected obedience but were not oppressive. To one of the younger sisters the mother appeared to be a matriarchal figure and the father a kind of clan chieftain, whose arrival at the evening meal instantly produced good behavior on the part of the little ones. He was less remote with his older children. As he was deaf in one ear, owing to a Fourth of July prank by some of his fellow citizens in his bachelor days, Jeannette and Wellington were always seated at table closest to his "good" ear so that he could converse with them during the meal.

There was the normal amount of squabbling among the children at home, but should any of them be attacked by a child outside the clan, they formed a solid phalanx in defense of their own, striking terror in the heart of the assailant. For the most part they were free to wander and explore and experiment on the ranch, and this they did even when curiosity led them into areas that were strictly forbidden. The sawmill was one of these, because its exposed machinery made it dangerous for the little ones; nevertheless, the children often slipped away to watch it in operation when their father was engaged elsewhere. They also knew instinctively what discoveries might be frowned on by their conventional Victorian parents, and kept mum about the time they had watched a sow farrow her piglets, all six of them.

John Rankin had great respect for the intelligence of his oldest daughter and from her early years gave her confidence in her own judgment. On one occasion he bought a machine to hoist hay into the barn and was giving it a trial run when the whole creaking contrivance got stuck. As he was busy trying to control a fairly wild team, he could not see what had gone wrong, and the hired hands seemed equally mystified. Jeannette, then a child of eight or nine, was standing nearby, fascinated by the scene, and pointed out the obstruction in the works to her father. She was right. "Aren't you ashamed," he chided the gawking men, "to have a little girl tell you what you ought to know?"

Of all the animals on the ranch, the horses were naturally the most important and the most interesting to the children. Like their elders they had to learn the different traits and idiosyncrasies of the beasts on whom life or health might depend. Some were reliable under any circumstances; others were more temperamental, but aroused special affection in the Rankin family either because of their beauty or because of a streak of willfulness and a tendency to clown. Jeannette learned to ride when very young, not as a sport but as a way of getting around, riding sidesaddle, as did all women of that period. She knew too that any injury to a horse must be looked after promptly, lest the horse become disabled. Once when she was no more than twelve years old, she saw one of the cowhands riding up to the ranch on a horse with a bad cut on its shoulder, the flesh hanging loose and bleeding from a wound incurred on a barbed wire fence. She bade the man stop and get help to throw the horse, while she ran into the house for her sewing kit and hot water; returning quickly, she did a neat suture of the torn flesh.

On another occasion one of the ranch dogs caught its foot in a trap, and there was nothing to be done but to amputate the crushed member. Jeannette did this with considerable sangfroid, and when the foot healed she made a little leather boot to fit over the stump, which the dog wore to the end of his life.

Although they were a self-sufficient family, the Rankins never lacked for the society of neighbors and friends either on the ranch or in town. Both parents were extremely sociable and loved to have people around them. (One friend, Louise MacDonald, a schoolteacher in the town, occupied a room in the Missoula house for twenty-five years; she was such a fixture that the younger children were surprised to learn at her death that she was not a blood relative.) Since the distance between ranches was too great for casual visiting, the country house would often be filled with overnight or long-staying guests: friends, relatives, even mere acquaintances. Larger groups got together frequently for a barn dance. As the descendant of Scotsmen, John Rankin came naturally by his flying feet, and Jeannette remembers with what agility he could leap into the air and click his heels together twice before landing lightly on his toes. The jollity of a country dance frequently spurred the young men to play practical jokes, as when Jeannette's Uncle Duncan, seeing a row of sleeping babies wrapped in identifying blankets along one wall of the barn, exchanged a pair of them. In their fatigue and in the dim light of the lanterns, the babies' parents selected their infants according to where they had placed them, and drove for many miles toward home before discovering this error. In his novel *The Virginian*, Owen Wister describes just such an incident of crude frontier humor, which the Rankins long believed was based on Uncle Duncan's youthful caper.

In the town, the social life of the Rankins, unlike that of many of their neighbors, was not centered on the church. John Rankin was by lineage a Presbyterian, but Mrs. Rankin, brought up as a Congregationalist, did not like to leave her home on Sunday mornings (who else would cook the Sunday midday dinner?), so the family never attended services. The children, however, were permitted to go to Sunday school, where they enjoyed hearing Bible stories in an atmosphere somewhat more permissive and relaxed than ruled in the daily classroom. Their enjoyment of these religious exercises was spiced by their great-uncle Bill Berry, an avowed atheist, who brought them a book illustrated with pictures of Presbyterians pitching babies into the fires of Hell because they hadn't been baptized. The youngsters pored over this volume in secret, knowing instinctively that it would not have been approved by their parents. Great-uncle Bill Berry, who had brought their mother to Missoula, was the type of Westerner who might have figured in frontier stories by Mark Twain. As a young man he had taken part in the gold rush to California in 1849 and had later been one of the earliest settlers in Missoula. His prominence in local affairs won him election as sheriff, a post he held for many years and which entitled him to lodgings in the county courthouse. He grew so attached to his quarters that even after he "ran out of votes," as Jeannette remembered, he refused to leave, and since no one dared put him out, he lived there until he died.

On summer evenings, when the ranchhouse had a full complement of visitors like Uncle Bill, the children listened goggle-eyed to heated discussions of local politics, anecdotes of the gold rush and early settlement in Montana, as well as blood-curdling tales of Indian warfare. There were many southerners among the ranchers, men ready to fight the Civil War all over again, at least in conversation. But of all the talk the most absorbing to the young ones concerned the Indians, whose strange presence in their world was only dimly understood. They were accustomed to seeing parties of Indians riding past the house in Missoula, the men on horseback, dragging travois poles attached to a platform that carried their tools and provisions, the women straggling behind on foot. The Rankin children were also permitted to attend the great Indian ceremonials and took pride in learning the simple ritual steps of the dances and memorizing the songs that accompanied them. Looking back on her long struggle for women's rights, Jeannette would sometimes say she wished she had given her energies to the cause of the Indians rather than to feminism.

In much of the West at that period the Indians still seemed to pose a threat to white settlement. In 1876, only four years before Jeannette was born, General Custer had engaged the Sioux at Little Big Horn and had been massacred along with his entire battalion of 264 men. Within a year of that event, however, Federal troops forced the surrender of some 5,000 Indians, and the Montana settlers thought themselves secure in possession of their lands. What seemed to be a new threat appeared in the fall of 1877, when the Nez Percés, under Chief Joseph, entered the territory after a masterly retreat of more than 1,700 miles from Idaho. In Idaho they had been confined to a reservation by the terms of a treaty with the United States which they claimed had been violated, and it was their intention now to cross over into Canada. On receipt of news that Chief Joseph and the Nez Percés had reached the Lolo Pass where it enters the Bitter Root Valley (their old hunting grounds), Captain Charles Rawn, the commander of the local garrison, sent word that every white man in the district who owned a gun was to join him and his few regulars and set up a barricade to intercept the Indians.

John Rankin had a gun and, according to his son Wellington, was always ready for a fight, so he joined up. At the opening of the pass, Rawn set up the barricade, then sent word to Chief Joseph: "Surrender your arms or you'll cross here over our dead bodies." Surrendering their arms would have meant that the Indians had no means of obtaining the game they needed for food in their passage to Canada. Chief Joseph, who came to be known as the wisest and most pacific of Indian leaders, answered: "We'll cross the mountains, and not over any dead bodies." As John Rankin told his children, Captain Rawn returned to his "troops" and laid out a plan of action: at dawn the next day they were to fall on the Indians, shoot them, and take their guns away from them, whatever the cost. At break of day, therefore, the settlers sallied forth, only to find that in the dead of night Chief Joseph had led his people around Rawn's lines, over a hill, and into the Bitter Root Valley without firing a shot.

The Nez Percés never made it to Canada. Surrounded by greatly superior forces in Chouteau County, exhausted after their long march, without provisions at the beginning of winter, their numbers reduced by the massacre of their braves, their women and their children, they surrendered at last. But ever since then the spot where Captain Rawn set up his barricade and submitted his ultimatum has been known in Montana as "Fort Fizzle." One of Jeannette's sisters believes that it was this story that made Jeannette a lifelong pacifist. And Jeannette herself, in repeating it, always added that the incident gave her father the dim view of the military mind which she came to share.

But the Fort Fizzle happening occurred before she was born, and thus it lacked the immediacy of a more gruesome event that took place when she was old enough to sense its horror. At an Indian mission not far from Missoula, an Indian boy got drunk on the white man's liquor and began making a nuisance of himself. The brave regulars made a foray on the mission and shot every man, woman and child on the spot.

A happier incident that Jeannette liked to recall directly involved one of her classmates at the high school in Missoula. This boy was looked on almost with awe by his contemporaries because of an event of which he was the unwitting hero. When still a baby he had crossed the plains with his parents in a covered wagon, one of a train of settlers who had camped one night in their usual fashion, in a circle, for defense against possibly hostile Indians. In the morning, to be sure, a cavalcade of Indians appeared on the horizon, and all the men in the party ran for their guns. The boy's mother, however, ran for her baby. Clasping him in her arms, she advanced toward the feathered chief. Then, to the dismay of her companions, she handed the child to the red man, babbling that he was her first child. The Indians could not understand what she said, but they could see that this was the most precious thing she possessed and that she trusted them; moreover, they had never seen a white baby at such close range before. They passed the infant from hand to hand in wonderment before returning him to his mother. Then they rode away.

Life on the ranch was so enjoyable that the family's return to Missoula in the fall was always a letdown, mitigated only to a degree by the diversions of the rapidly growing town. In 1883 the Northern Pacific Railroad came to Missoula, as Henry Villard forged the last link in a system that was to link the eastern half of the country with the Pacific Northwest. For the private train loaded with dignitaries (including the President of the United States) which stopped at Missoula on its way to the ceremony of the Golden Spike, the town prepared a great celebration—as great, that is, as its sparse population could mount. Jeannette was only three years old at the time, but the event was frequently recalled among her elders, and its importance in joining the town to the outside world was long remembered. When she was nine, even more joyous festivities signaled the admission of Montana to statehood. After the railroad came the horse cars, which made travel within the expanding town more convenient, and Jeannette and her brother and sisters used to take delight after a heavy snowfall in seeing the horses bypass the tracks and haul the cars from side to side along the streets wherever they could find a footing.

Returning to Missoula meant returning to school, which she found a dreadful bore. To her quick and eager mind, learning by rote was a waste of time, which may have led her, later in life, to interest herself in various projects of progressive education. On the ranch she learned without effort, simply by doing things, by being exposed to problems and solving them pragmatically. Whatever else she may have learned in school, she never learned to spell. When she went to high school she played basketball, but a broken nose suffered in one game ended what had never been a real involvement in competitive sports. She loved ice-skating, although the swift changes in the climate of western Montana made the season for this uncertain. A brief membership in a girls' club called the "Buds" failed to arouse her interest; she found their activities rather silly and childish compared with the lively sociability of her home.

And at home there was almost never a dull or an idle moment. Like most women of her time Mrs. Rankin had one child after another; four beginning in 1880, then an interval of four years marked by successive miscarriages, followed by three more births. In consequence the three surviving eldest, Jeannette, Harriet and Wellington, were regarded by the three youngest as almost of another generation. As she grew into her teens Jeannette was charged with more and more responsibility for the little ones, for with only limited hired help Mrs. Rankin had all she could do to manage the household and cook for her family and guests. In a way, therefore, because of her role as a surrogate mother, Jeannette could be said to have had children, although she never married. Edna, the baby of the family, once remarked that Jeannette sometimes looked at her as if she were an unwanted child. The youngest of large families often have this feeling of being superfluous, unless, as sometimes happens, they are petted to the point of believing themselves to be indispensable.

Both parents, at any rate, recognized Jeannette's resourcefulness and dependability. There was a special tie, however, between the girl and her father, for he saw in her a reflection of his own adventurous spirit and independence of mind. Although her mother had been a schoolteacher, Jeannette always turned to her father, limited as his formal education had been, for assistance in solving arithmetic problems that stumped her. Jeannette for her part took great interest in John Rankin's multifarious affairs. One of his more daring enterprises after the coming of the railroad to Missoula was the building of what came to be known as "the Rankin block" on Front Street, a brick edifice three stories high, housing shops and offices and a hotel of sixty-five rooms. Jeannette was understandably quite proud of this achievement. On one occasion Mr. Rankin was about to sell a property he owned in the town when he found that the purchaser would not close the deal because there was no sidewalk in front of the building. Jeannette undertook to lay the sidewalk herself and thus made it possible for her father to complete the sale. In those days Missoula's sidewalks were made of wooden planks, not stone or cement, but still the incident shows how attentively Jeannette had observed her father and others do jobs of carpentry. Laying a sidewalk was a lot more fun than sitting around in your best dress at the tea parties of the "Buds." It gave you something to stand on.

As she grew into her teens she sought or was given other outlets for her latent energies. Her mother gave her a few simple lessons in sewing so that Jeannette could make her own dolls' clothes, whereupon the girl soon became an expert seamstress, making all her sisters' dresses from the age of thirteen on. Emboldened by her success in this field, one day she decided to go into business, and Mrs. Rankin, at first taken aback when a passerby stopped in and asked for the dressmaker whose sign was prominently displayed in an upstairs window, dismissed the inquiry with a shake of the head. "Oh, that must be Jeannette's idea," she answered, as if to say that anything might be expected from that quarter.

Every year as the school term drew to a close, the prospect of the summer to come began to fill the sleeping and waking hours of the young Rankins. Some days, or sometimes weeks, before school was dismissed, they received special permission from the authorities to take off for the ranch. Perched in the surrey, or later, as their numbers increased, piled into a hayrack with all their gear, they drove the six miles out into the country, to the larger life under the big sky. It was at the ranch, Jeannette said long afterward, that she did her "thinking," thinking that may have been no more than the vague humanitarian ideas and unformed longings of an adolescent to begin with, which, as she grew older, sought an outlet in some practical expression of good faith. It was at the ranch, for example, that she first came to realize that there might be some injustice in the economic system and, as Wellington recalled, complained to her father about the arduous working conditions of the ranch hands.

Back to town again in the autumn, as the years went by, she prepared to enter the University of Montana, which was due to open in Missoula in 1898. But before she went to college she had already exhibited some of those traits that were to serve her so well throughout her life: a passion to observe and learn things for herself, an enjoyment of nature and of people, a strong sympathy for the underdog, and above all a willingness to undertake any task that promised to be interesting. It never occurred to her that some of the tasks she set herself were considered "man's work," any more than she downgraded the "woman's work" she was obliged to do. It was all part of the world's work, and in her girlhood she indicated her readiness to seize any opportunity for action that presented itself, even to make the opportunity, if need be. She had sharpened her wits in a friendly sibling rivalry, for her brother and sisters were capable, intelligent persons almost all of whom were to make their mark. Her parents too had given her some things without which she could not have survived to use her talents and energy as well as she did: humane values, a sturdy physique, and a sense of humor to bear with the disappointments of a life of action.

II

Go! Go! Go!

In a journal Jeannette kept before she entered college she wrote an exhortation to herself: "Go! Go! Go!" The destination she had in mind was vague, but the anxiety to be on the move—and not merely physically—was persistent, and later in her life proved to be chronic. For most of the decade following her graduation from high school, however, she was to remain bound to Montana, summering at the ranch, wintering in Missoula, unable to break away into a wider world for any length of time.

The four years she spent at Montana State University in Missoula were a disappointment to her; living at home, she could not enjoy the novelty of a change of scene, or contact with young people of other backgrounds and interests, while in the classrooms of that raw college few courses seemed to fire her imagination or exercise the muscles of her mind. Her exact contemporary Frances Perkins, after attending a prestigious woman's college in the East, also affirmed that she never learned to use her mind until she went to graduate school.

In those days students did not clamor for "relevance" in their college curriculum as they do today, nor could girls rightly have explained to what the curriculum should have been relevant—to marriage and motherhood, to housework and entertaining? Although Jeannette worked hard at her studies, they had little to do with her as yet formless strivings. Some of her professors described her as shy, but it is more likely that she was merely reserved. Out of affection for her biology teacher she wrote her senior essay on snails, a subject that promised no opening to a fruitful career. Unaware of any special gifts, she thought she would like to train as a nurse when she finished college, but her father, familiar with her independent spirit, dissuaded her from engaging in so narrow a profession.

Graduating in 1902 with a B.Sc., she found that she was qualified for nothing but teaching, and that only on the elementary level. She taught school briefly in Missoula, and then in Whitehall, a town near Butte, without winning a permanent certificate. That she failed to qualify as a teacher was perhaps due to her own expansive temperament, which chafed under the rigid educational practices of the time. Restless, and casting about for something to do, she worked for a period as an apprentice dressmaker, drawing on her experience as the family seamstress and showing a decided aptitude for dress-designing. About this time her sister Edna, then a child of nine or ten, needed a party dress in which to appear as a performer at the recital of the local piano teacher. Jeannette promised to make it for her but was so preoccupied that she never got around to it until the day before the recital. Edna was very apprehensive lest the costume reveal her bulging little tummy and was ready to burst into tears when Jeannette sewed a broad ruffle about the middle of the dress. To Edna the effect was disastrous. Jeannette, however, took one look at the child and without a word whipped out a length of moire ribbon and tied it around Edna's waist, leaving the ruffle to show only as an accent, a finishing touch that minimized the bulge and made Edna the most elegantly clad, if not necessarily the best performer, at the recital.

A little later, looking farther afield for more creative work, Jeannette took a correspondence course in furniture design. This too proved to be a dead end. She had already shown, and would demonstrate again and again, that she had a decided gift for mechanics. With training she might have become a builder or an architect, perhaps even an inventor, but the thought was never entertained either by her or by her advisers; it would have been foreign to all the myths and symbols about womanhood in those days. One summer evening at the ranch, for example, when the house was filled with young people, she took a group out to the sawmill, assigned them to various posts, and herself ran the complicated machinery to cut planks out of a huge log.

Around this time several young men came forward with proposals of marriage, but none awoke any passion in her or seemed likely to understand the needs of her temperament, and she refused them without regret. The fact that she never married did not mean that she was hostile to the other sex; on the contrary she enjoyed the company of men and had many loyal men friends throughout her life. She saw no reason for giving up her independence merely for the married state, and as for wanting a family of her own, the family she was born into provided sufficient outlet for her maternal instincts in the younger siblings she was required to look after. Furthermore, when she went out into the world to make her own career, she transferred all those biological urges to a larger sphere without losing any of her deeply feminine qualities.

The two men who figured most significantly in her life were her father and her brother, and in 1904 her father suddenly died of Rocky Mountain spotted fever. As her relations with her father had been very close, it was a cruel blow to lose him at a moment when she needed his counsel and support so much, but on the other hand his death set her free to make her own decisions and find her own way without parental restraint, since her mother had such respect for Jeannette's intelligence and capability that she always deferred to her eldest daughter.

John Rankin left his family an estate of between $100,000 and $150,000, a tidy fortune in those days, which assured them of a competence, as well as funds for the education of all the children. With five still to be supported through college, however, the Rankins were obliged to be thrifty in other areas. As Jeannette told an interviewer a few years ago, people in the town used to say that "the Rankins never could afford anything in the house," but "could always afford a railroad ticket to go East. . . . We had nice furniture when we moved in, but after that we never could have anything new because we were always so busy buying education."*

The first ticket to go East was purchased for Wellington (then aged twenty), who after a few years at the state university went on to Harvard for another B.A., then to Oxford in England for a period, returning to Harvard again for his law degree. It never occurred to John or Olive Rankin that Jeannette too might have profited by this type of higher education, nor did she for the moment aspire to it. Wellington was a bright, personable young man as well as the family pet, and she was eager for him to get a broader view of the world than Montana offered. In this matter she not only played the role of the adoring mother who wants her child to have "advantages" greater than her own; she also felt close enough in spirit and sympathy to Wellington to know that he would share much of what he learned and experienced with her.

In 1904, after the death of her father, she made her first trip alone out of the state to visit Wellington at Harvard and relatives of her mother in Boston. Her curiosity about the rest of the world had long gone unsatisfied; now at last she was to indulge an appetite for travel that was to last all her life without ever being fully appeased. The experience was stimulating, but it was also shattering, for in Boston, for the first time, she came face to face with a big-city slum where masses of human beings lived crowded together in conditions of unimaginable poverty and squalor, the children undernourished and uncared for, and their elders work-worn or unemployed and spiritless. Nothing in Montana had prepared her for this. In the West, cases of poverty were not visible in the mass, save for the Indians.

Fifteen years earlier Jane Addams had had a similar awakening when she saw the wretchedness of the London East End (not much altered from the baneful scenes described by Dickens long before) and realized that in her native Chicago, beyond the periphery of her own sheltered life, the same conditions must exist. Learning now what the founder of Hull House was trying

* When she made this statement Jeannette neglected to tell of how after her father's death she had drawn up the plans and supervised the addition of a bedroom and bath on the first floor, adjacent to the dining room.

to do to mitigate those conditions, Jeannette began reading avidly the current literature of protest: the muckraking magazines, the works of Jacob Riis, Jack London, Henry George, and particularly anything she could lay hands on by or about Miss Addams.

On her return to Montana, these new perspectives deepened her discontent as she began to make what in today's fashionable terminology is called "a search for identity." In her mother's house, to be sure, there were still many chores for an unmarried daughter to assume, and in the town she was known as a responsible citizen who could be called upon to act in an emergency or perform some civic duty. In 1907, for example, a train engineer got in touch with her to say that he was obliged to drop a little orphan boy at the station. Because of some carelessness in the arrangements, the child, who was being sent to a farm at some distance, had not been able to change to the proper train and would be unattended, without food or lodging, unless someone could be found to look after him. Jeannette promptly went down to the station to find the boy, put him up at a hotel, saw to it that he was fed, and arranged for his transportation the next day to the farmer who was to take him in.

But although she was occupied, there were reserves of energy and vitality in Jeannette that were going unused, and it is not surprising that in her frustration she should begin to feed on herself, to feel out of sorts, and at last to become really ill. Seeking a more salutary climate (although it was not so much the physical as the social climate of Missoula that caused her to languish), the following year she went to San Francisco, presumably for her health. Here she took up residence for four months at a settlement house called the Telegraph Hill Association. This was her first real breakaway from Montana.

Now twenty-eight years old, she felt that she had found her vocation at last as a social worker, a career that would enable her to be of use to people, more rewarding by far than nursing or teaching or any other area in which she had made false starts. In order to qualify herself further for this new occupation, she went to New York the next fall to enroll in the New York School of Philanthropy, forerunner of the Columbia University School of Social Work.

In the director of the School, Pauline Goldmark, and in its faculty, Jeannette found the moral and intellectual stimulation to give focus to her aspirations. Her school work required her to spend two months in the night courts (the scene of police roundups of prostitutes), two months studying the needs and problems of deaf children, and two months in general charity work. Since all this was interesting to her, she earned high marks. The daily spectacle of how the poor and the underprivileged lived deepened her sense of the social injustices in the American economic system, which she had felt vaguely even as a girl, and which had been confirmed during her trip to Boston and her stay in San Francisco.

Could she apply some of her new-found techniques of social welfare to Missoula? By this time Missoula had grown to the point where it had a few of the less glamorous attributes of an American city, although it called itself "The Garden City of the Treasure State," or less frequently, "The Gate of the Golden West, the Gem of the Mountains," and boasted of thirteen churches, a literary society, several banks, a new courthouse, a new bridge and a new theater! It needed no very diligent search on Jeannette's part, however, to discover on her return home that there was room for improvement in certain areas. One day soon after the Fourth of July she went over to look into conditions in the town jail. The current sheriff, being an old friend of the Rankin family, readily gave her access to the prisoners' quarters, which she found so crowded with drunks, whores and other delinquents that men and women had been thrown together into common cells. On investigation she learned that these highly informal arrangements were due not only to the usual holiday highjinks, but more particularly because the deputy sheriff's large family occupied a sizable portion of the jail building. Jeannette reported these facts to some of the leading women in town, and the matter was brought up in court. When the judge asked the sheriff to describe conditions in the jail, the sheriff tried to pass the whole thing off by saying that there was no problem; Jeannette Rankin had cooked it all up. "Well, then," asked the judge, "why are all the good women in town telephoning me about it?" Unlike Jeannette's Great-Uncle Bill Berry, the deputy sheriff's family was evicted from the jail and had to find other lodgings.*

She had less success in trying to establish an employment bureau and set up a public bath. Missoula did not in fact seem to offer much opportunity for a social worker; it was too new, there was little hereditary poverty, and there was still some flow among the economic strata. In the fall of 1910, therefore, she accepted the offer of a job in a children's home in Spokane, Washington, hoping that here at last was the opening she had sought. This too proved to be a dead end: she found conditions in the home "appalling" but dared not make an issue of it, because if she did the children would just be moved to an institution just as bad, or perhaps even worse. The narrow routine of the home, moreover, was suffocating. She quit after a few weeks and, unwilling to go back to Missoula and admit defeat, enrolled for courses at the University of Washington in Seattle. Her studies here—economics, sociology, public speaking—indicated a new range of interests, more contemporary and more relevant than those of her undergraduate years.

And now, after eight years of floundering and seeking, Jeannette was about to find her footing and her direction. Here in the state of Washington, in the year 1910, the people were to go to the polls in November to vote on an amendment granting woman suffrage, an issue with which Jeannette was in complete sympathy, even though she had never before seen how she could participate in bringing it about. The time and the place were now

* More space in the jail was needed late that same summer, when Elizabeth Gurley Flynn (then nineteen years old, and pregnant), her husband Jack Jones, and a man named Frank Little came to Missoula to organize lumber workers and migrant laborers on behalf of the International Workers of the World—the Wobblies—whose syndicalist principles had begun to arouse grave apprehensions among the respectables of the West. Every time these radicals tried to hold a street meeting they were arrested, all but Elizabeth, and in order to keep the issue of free speech alive she kept sending for more agitators to take the place of those in jail. At length she too was put in the lockup, not in a common cell (in recognition of her pregnancy) but in the sheriff's own quarters. They were all released early in the fall, because the town officials did not want the publicity of a trial of free speech to draw attention from the imminent opening of the Apple Fair for which Missoula was renowned.

auspicious; moreover, she was prepared in every way to contribute her services. On her own initiative she obtained a batch of suffrage posters and volunteered to place them in all the shop windows. This action won the interest of the suffrage leaders, who promptly invited her to go out into the field to canvass voters. She accepted the offer with some trepidation, for she was totally inexperienced in political legwork; it seemed to her that she was sent to the most difficult spots, towns where she felt she made no impression whatever.

"I was sent to Ballard," she wrote later, "and worked for two days to get a meeting place, distribute leaflets, put up posters: seven people came to listen and talk. . . . It was only later that I could confess my early frustration to others, but when I did, one of the Seattle women said, 'After we saw what you could do *in Ballard*, we *knew* we could use you.' " That the suffragists showed such understanding of her efforts gave her confidence—a confidence that was reinforced when the suffrage amendment won out in the November elections.

She could not have made her start in the suffrage movement under better tutelage. The women who directed the Washington campaign—Emma Smith Devoe, May Arkwright and Abigail Smith Duniway—were extremely able organizers. From them Jeannette learned that in order to swing an election, every district, every county, every precinct in a state must be canvassed; committees must be set up locally and workers assigned to learn the attitude of every voter; and the activities of all the local committees must be coordinated under a central committee to keep track of developments all over. Beyond this the Washington leaders were astute political tacticians: one of their precepts was not to waste time arguing with the already converted; you just put them to work. Another expedient was to have the proposed constitutional amendment phrased in such general terms that the right to vote was granted to both sexes without using the words "woman" or "female" in the text. (Many men who voted for the amendment said later that they would never have approved it if they had known they were giving women the right to vote!) Still another point stressed in the Washington campaign finds a late echo among the most intelligent women's liberation advocates, that men be brought to understand that women did not want the vote "in a spirit of warfare," but "in the spirit of harmony and interdependence between men and women."

Thus Jeannette served her apprenticeship in a very practical school, learning how a political campaign was organized, what planning, what staff, what approach to the people were needed. She had made her contribution to a cause she could cherish, and above all she had had a taste—a slight taste, to be sure—of that delicious intoxicant, success. If she could be useful in Washington, couldn't she be even more effective in her home state?

In December 1910 she left Seattle to spend the Christmas holidays with her family in Missoula, and while there learned from the newspapers that a suffrage amendment was to be introduced in the legislature at Helena at the next session, opening in January of the new year. Suffrage amendments had been periodically offered in Montana since 1902 and had been regularly rejected. They had been regarded as something of a farce, comic relief for the tedium of the serious business debated by the people's representatives, calling for sparkling displays of wit.

On a sudden impulse Jeannette decided to jolt these wags into a more respectful attitude toward the issue, and in a daring move she sent word that she would like to address the legislature on the subject, in the name of the Equal Franchise Society. She herself had hastily organized this society in the state capital when she discovered that no suffrage groups existed there. An invitation to appear before the House on February 1 was duly extended to her—not that the legislators thought anything would come of it, but perhaps as a courtesy due the high repute of the Rankin family in Montana affairs, perhaps because it would allow the professional jokesters a chance for more good clean fun.

The occasion was made something of a fete. Members of the Senate did not attend the sitting of the House officially but adjourned their own session and came in force to listen to Miss Rankin's speech. The chamber was filled to capacity when she made her appearance; women were seated on the platform for the first time in Montana's history; men pressed in at the doorways; vases of live flowers bedecked the hall, in keeping with the nodding plumes and floral trimmings on the hats of the women in

Miss Rankin in 1911, when she addressed the Montana legislature to urge passage of a suffrage amendment.

Montana Historical Society

the galleries. House members had each put up fifty cents to provide the flowers and had voted to ban cigars, spittoons and other signs of male occupancy.

Jeannette was introduced with much gallantry. She was understandably nervous, for it was the first time in her life that she had addressed a large audience, as well as the first time any woman had come to speak before the Montana lawgivers. Her speech had been carefully prepared and memorized, under the coaching of Wellington, who was now a rising young lawyer in Helena, but she almost forgot what she was going to say, she recalled later, when the audience fervently applauded her opening statement that she had been born in Montana. Not too many of those present could boast of being native sons or daughters. Gathering her wits, she spoke earnestly and to good effect, setting forth all the reasons why women should have the vote and pointing out that suffrage had already been adopted in some of the most enlightened countries in the world. In her conclusion she showed that she understood the constitutional problem as well: "We are not asking you gentlemen to decide this great question," she said. "We are merely asking you to leave it to the voters."

When she had finished there was another great round of applause, and Representative Binnard, the most determined opponent of suffrage in the House, rose and proffered her a bouquet of violets. This condescending gesture was not lost on Jeannette, who wanted votes, not violets. When the amendment came to a vote later in the session, it was clear that her speech had had a good effect, for the measure won a majority in the House, short of the two-thirds needed to submit the amendment to the electorate, but enough to give promise of success in later sessions. It was an auspicious beginning for Jeannette; her speech won wide publicity, her name became known throughout the state, and she had made woman suffrage a live issue in Montana.

Within the space of only a few months she had discovered what she was fitted for: the art of politics, a metier more exciting, more fulfilling than any she had imagined, and one that drew on every talent, every discipline, every belief that she possessed. She now knew where she was going.

III

Votes for Women

The American woman suffrage movement received its original impetus from a characteristic instance of male chauvinism. At an international antislavery convention held in London in 1840, the female delegates who had been most active among the Abolitionists in the United States and elsewhere were denied the right to sit on the floor of the meeting hall but were relegated to the galleries, where they could hear but not participate in the discussions. This arbitrary act of discrimination led Lucretia Mott, a leading Abolitionist, and others to ask themselves whether the condition of women was not analogous to that of the chattel slaves, and prompted them to call the first women's rights convention in Seneca Falls in 1848. At this and subsequent conventions the whole range of disabilities under which women suffered was aired without animosity toward the other sex, almost as if the mere recital of their wrongs could bring correction.

As the irrepressible conflict approached, however, in 1860, conceding that Negro slavery represented the greater injustice, the women subordinated their claims until after the Civil War. On the passage of the Fourteenth Amendment to the Constitution in 1867, an amendment that defined a citizen as a male, the women once again were reminded of their role as second-class persons. All their male collaborators in the Abolitionist movement—Charles Sumner, William Lloyd Garrison, Wendell Phillips and Frederick Douglass—had joined with Republican politicians of the most cynical partisan views in urging this amendment, justifying their position by saying that this was the Negro's hour; the woman's hour would come later.

Disheartened by this betrayal on the part of their friends, the women came to see that their first goal in the fight for social equality must be the right to vote, the elimination of the sex barrier to full citizenship. In 1869 two organizations were formed to achieve this purpose: the National Woman Suffrage Association, which urged the passage of an amendment to the Federal Constitution; and the American Woman Suffrage Association, which pressed for amendments to the constitutions of all the states. Despite the tireless efforts of such dedicated women as Lucy Stone, Susan B. Anthony, Elizabeth Cady Stanton, and Anna Howard Shaw, the movement made little progress. The two groups joined forces in 1890, under the redundant name of the National American Woman Suffrage Association, but it was not until 1905, when Carrie Chapman Catt took over the leadership, that they began to get under way in earnest, operating on both the state and Federal levels. Mrs. Catt, a brilliant organizer, conceived and set up a wide network of state and local groups down to the precincts along the lines of a national political party, staffed by thousands of volunteer workers, and using every device of persuasion and publicity employed by the most sophisticated political machine workers.

Mrs. Catt's tactics had borne fruit in the state of Washington in 1910. The Washington victory was interpreted as a breakthrough in that it was the first state with large city populations that had been won for suffrage; the others—Wyoming, Colorado, Idaho and Utah—had been predominantly rural in character. Washington, however, was only the fifth state in the union to grant women the vote, and if the war was to be won on state lines, there were still forty-three more battles to be won. The Federal Constitution, the citadel, seemed light-years away from capture.*

* How difficult this might be had been illustrated when Wyoming Territory had applied for statehood; its territorial constitution having been the first to allow woman suffrage, the same clause was included in its state constitution;

Still there was a great wave of optimism throughout the suffrage movement as new approaches to the problem and new leaders sprang up. Jeannette Rankin's activities in Washington State and in Montana did not escape the notice of suffrage leaders elsewhere. In May 1911 she returned to New York City, having been offered a job with the New York Woman Suffrage Party by its head, Harriet Laidlaw, with whom she had become friendly in the course of her earlier stay. Whereas in Washington she had worked in the rural districts and in small towns, now she confronted the more knowledgeable citizenry of the metropolis.

The propaganda technique used was common enough in that era; the only uncommon factor was that women were making the pitch. As Jeannette recalled, she and her colleagues would wait on a street corner until some pleasant-looking people came along, when they would say: "Will you please stand for a few minutes?" These few would attract others and make an audience, whereupon the suffragists would get up on their soap boxes and begin their spiel. Jeannette had to learn to think fast on her feet and be ready for a soft but apt answer to passing toughs. Soliciting signatures for petitions, she even nerved herself to enter bars and cafes, behavior that would have raised eyebrows in respectable Montana circles.

But here she chafed under the instructions of her superiors in the movement, who bade her obtain as many signatures as possible in favor of a suffrage amendment to the state constitution, by whatever means. The technique she was advised to follow was to hand around a petition bearing the name of a local political boss, whose influence was so great that the pages were quickly filled up by the boss's loyal henchmen with no idea of what they were signing. Preferring to make converts by earnest argument, Jeannette often returned to headquarters with only three or four signatures.

Working in the suffrage movement in New York brought her into contact with a galaxy of brilliant women who shared her indignation and passion for reform. Among them was Elisabeth

---

and there was fierce and prolonged debate in Congress as to whether statehood should be granted to a territory with such bizarre electoral provisions.

Irwin, who had studied at the New York School of Philanthropy and like Jeannette had been an observer at the night courts, and who later became known as the founder of the Little Red Schoolhouse, one of the pioneer projects for progressive education. Other intimates were Cornelia Swinnerton and Mary Beard, wife of the historian Charles Beard, a scholar in her own right and an active participant in various reform movements. The warmest and most lasting friendship Jeannette formed at this time was with Katharine Anthony, a gifted writer who not long afterward won recognition as the author of witty and learned biographies.

It was a stirring period, when women were beginning to sense their own capabilities, to make judgments not only about their own status but about the problems of society in general, and to venture to do something about them. Elisabeth Irwin gathered together a little group calling itself the Dinner Club, which held weekly meetings in her tiny apartment in Patchin Place in Greenwich Village. The club members were all high-spirited women, without solemnity, full of wit and humor, accomplished but not pretentious. They provided the liveliest sort of society that Jeannette had as yet encountered, and she entered into their discussions of human affairs with gusto. To her the most striking traits they shared were the ability and the will to make a place for themselves as persons in areas where women had rarely operated before, often where few of either sex had been engaged. Meeting these spirited women was a heady draught for Jeannette, who had felt within herself powers that had not been used and a drive that had had no direction.

Though their talents led them along different paths, all were agreed on the necessity of changing the status of women. They were not only suffragists; they were feminists. A few years later Katharine Anthony was to characterize the feminist movement as "the restoration of women's self-respect," a phrase that is a commonplace today. Women must learn, she wrote, not to depreciate their own sex. "The individual woman is required . . . a thousand times a day to choose either to accept her appointed role and thereby rescue her good disposition out of the wreckage of her self-respect, or else follow an independent line of behavior and rescue her self-respect out of the wreckage of her

Katharine Anthony, Miss Rankin's lifelong friend.

good disposition." Jeannette had had ample opportunity to observe the truth of this.

In Elisabeth Irwin's little sitting room they talked about woman suffrage, equal pay for equal work, equal access to education and to jobs for which they were qualified, legal protection of motherhood and childhood within and outside of marriage, day care centers for working mothers and payment to mothers who chose to take care of their own children, birth control, even the right to have an abortion. Perhaps the least important if the most immediate item in the feminist calendar was the vote. It was widely believed at the time that all those other advances would follow naturally and in due course as a result of woman suffrage. Suffrage was the first stronghold to be stormed by the activists.

From this time forward, having shown her mettle in the wars of suffrage, Jeannette was assigned to one battlefield after another. In the fall of 1911, again through the good offices of

Harriet Laidlaw, she was appointed a member of the Central Committee of the California Progressive Party, which was urging the adoption of a suffrage amendment in California that year. Jeannette went to work in the rural and semirural districts, where she felt quite at home. On one occasion she was sent up to the north of the state to a town that could be reached only by stage-coach, and while the conveyance was rattling along the dirt roads she fell into conversation with another passenger, who turned out to be the local school superintendent. At one point he told her that the school in the town she was heading for had an all-girl band. "Why only girls?" she asked. "Because they're more reliable," he answered. "They come to practice." And so when she gave her suffrage speech on the main street, she asked the all-girl band to play for her, thus attracting a good audience. The campaign was a lively one all over the state, and though suffrage won by only a small majority, it was gratifying to Jeannette that the favorable rural vote swung the balance.

Having proved her worth to the movement once more, on returning to New York she was sent to Albany in January 1912 to lobby for a suffrage amendment there. Albany that season was thronged with social workers, some of whom Jeannette had been acquainted with earlier. Frances Perkins was at the state capital, lobbying for the 54-hour bill for women workers, along with Rose Schneiderman, Florence Kelley and many others who had come forward in the aftermath of the Triangle Shirtwaist Company fire the preceding year, when 146 girls lost their lives, to urge passage of regulatory and safety measures. In fact the current of reform was so strong that there seemed to be hope for a suffrage amendment as well.

Jeannette succeeded in having a resolution favoring votes for women introduced in the Senate, but it did not pass. One of the senators she approached was young Franklin D. Roosevelt, whom Jeannette and her colleagues found insufferably callow and patronizing at the time. When she told him that many western states were adopting suffrage, he replied that that might be very well in the West, a good idea, in fact, but things that worked in the West probably wouldn't work in the East. While she had his ear she tried also to win him over to pending legislation for the eight-hour day for women and children, but he was not sympathetic to that either. He explained that he spent his summers in Maine, and that in the port near his home a great blast on a horn was the signal that a fishing boat was coming in. At the sound of the horn all the women and children in the village would run down to the wharf to process the cargo, working without rest for as many hours as were required before the fish could spoil. "Well," said Jeannette, "if women were asked about that problem, they might decide that perhaps the *children* might spoil."

By now a seasoned traveler and agitator, she was next sent to Ohio, and then to Wisconsin, not registering much success in either place but gaining broader experience. In addition to making friends and studying political currents in any area, suffragists had to familiarize themselves with the laws and constitutions of the various states, which differed widely; of special importance were the mechanics of how a constitution could be amended. Jeannette made herself so useful in this and other ways that at the end of 1912 she was appointed field secretary of the National American Woman Suffrage Association, a job that entailed even more extended traveling about the country. The association was so well organized by now that train schedules, hotel reservations, public appearances and private meetings were arranged ahead of time, which left the field secretaries for the most part free to carry on their work without impediment.

Thus Jeannette was already known as one of the national leaders of the suffrage party when Wilson was elected president in November 1912. In the shift to the Democrats after sixteen years of Republican rule in Washington, the suffragists saw an opportunity to hold a great demonstration, hoping to impress the President, the Congress, and the people with the size and strength of their movement. It was to take the form of a mammoth parade on March 3, 1913, the day before Wilson's inauguration. Months were spent in preparation for this event, which was the brainchild of Alice Paul, a newcomer to the American suffrage movement but a veteran of the campaign in England, who had in fact worked beside the Pankhursts, and along with them had gone on a hunger strike when they were all sent to jail.

The plans called for a colorful procession of some five thou-

The great suffrage parade in Washington, D.C., in March 1913, as it started out. The scenes of violence that occurred later in the day were not photographed.

The Bettmann Archive, Inc.

sand women, led by the glamorous Inez Milholland* on horseback, carrying a trumpet with a purple banner, followed by an all-woman band, a mounted brigade, floats, marching contingents from all the states in local costume, and a long line of automobiles. It was to end with a tableau on the steps of the Treasury Building. In those days, before Americans became addicted to watching professional sports without even moving from their cozy living rooms, parades were a very popular form of mass entertainment, picturesque, enlivened by music, and free of charge. And like competitive sports today, they brought out the spirit of partisanship in every manly breast. The suffrage parade in Washington in 1913 was so well publicized that it promised to attract more spectators than the inauguration. In fact, as Woodrow Wilson was being driven from the Union Station that afternoon, on the eve of his installation as President of the United States, he asked why the streets along his way seemed so deserted. Was this a sign that he was not welcome

* Inez Milholland was an active suffragist, socialist and pacifist of the period; she was sometimes called the "Joan of Arc" of the feminist movement.

in the capital? "Oh, they're all watching the parade," he was told.

Jeannette had been appointed leader of the Montana delegation, whose members wore Indian costume and were to be headed by a girl dressed as Sacagawea, the squaw who had guided Lewis and Clark over the Great Divide in their exploration of the Northwest a hundred years earlier. The girl chosen for the role of Sacagawea was tall and dark, not unlike an Indian in appearance, but at the last moment she failed to appear. Her costume was on hand, however, and Jeannette, at her wits' end, could find no substitute but her sister Edna, who was fair and considerably shorter than the girl for whom the costume had been designed. In times of stress the Rankins always pressed one of their clan into service. Poor Edna had a miserable time of it as she marched down Pennsylvania Avenue, dragging her fringed apparel along the dirty pavement.

But Edna's troubles were as nothing compared to the experiences of other marchers in the parade. In spite of, or, as was evident later in the day, with the connivance of, the police, who were present in large numbers, unruly crowds did all they could to disrupt the procession. Even without the protection of hard hats, valiant men among the onlookers did not flinch from jeering and spitting at the marching women, slapping or tripping them up, throwing burning cigar stubs at them, shouting insults and obscenities. They pushed into the middle of the avenue so that the marchers were obliged to go two abreast instead of four, and at length in single file. Had not Alice Paul and other women driven their cars down the street to separate the crowds, many suffragists could not have passed at all. Rowdies seized and mauled young girls, and a gray-haired woman leading a college section was twice knocked down. When one marcher asked a policeman for help, he replied: "Oh, go home!" Another policeman answered the plea of a congressman's wife for protection with the gallant remark: "If my wife were where you are I'd break her head!"

The disorders were so serious that at length the army was called out, and a squad of the 15th Cavalry helped restore peace. After an investigation the chief of police was fired, but the women had learned, as decades later the peace protesters were to learn, that peaceful petition was only as peaceful as the keepers of the peace would allow it to be.*

For Jeannette the Washington parade was only a minor incident in a year of the most intense activity. Reporting to the convention of the National American Woman Suffrage Association toward the end of 1913, she described her multifarious operations, which included lobbying in the legislatures of Delaware, Florida, Tennessee, Alabama, Nebraska and South Dakota; a period of three weeks in Saginaw, Michigan, and five weeks in North Dakota to organize the suffrage campaigns there by ward and precinct and district; a trip by automobile from Montana to Washington, D.C., with petitions for a suffrage amendment to the constitution, in the course of which journey she stopped at thirty-three towns and cities for meetings. Having arrived in Washington, she remained there for two weeks interviewing southern congressmen on behalf of the amendment under the direction of Alice Paul, who headed the Congressional Union of the national association.

It was one of these southern congressmen, John Sharp Williams of Mississippi, who provided Jeannette with one of her favorite anecdotes of the suffrage struggle, a touching example of southern gallantry in conflict with the facts of life. Like Franklin Roosevelt, Williams conceded that suffrage might "work" in other places, but not in his home counties. "It's all right for you women in the North or the West, but we can't have it in the South because of the colored women." Jeannette, recalling the "grandfather clause" that effectively prevented black men from exercising their right to vote, answered him mischievously: "Can't you use the same methods against the Negro women that you use against the men?" Mr. Williams leaped to his feet in indignation. "You can't hit your baby's nurse over the head with a club!" he cried.

* By some curious lapse of memory which might interest a psychologist, neither Jeannette nor Alice Paul later in life had any recollection of the violence that marked the suffrage parade in Washington in 1913. The suppression of what might have been a traumatic experience for them is the more extraordinary in that both could recall with great exactitude many incidents of less dramatic impact over a period of almost three-quarters of a century.

Despite the frenetic pressure of these busy years, Jeannette had never lost touch with the situation in Montana. Immediately after her speech to the legislature in 1911 she had set up a two-fold program: to build an organization, and to inform the voters on the issue. A large part of her new-found confidence was due to her discovery that she had a natural aptitude for democratic politics and an instinctive grasp of devices whereby public opinion could be swayed. To begin with, she went quietly through the state, stopping in every county seat to search out women willing to help in the good work and to instruct them in how to set up equal franchise societies. Next she persuaded them to form a state central committee, of which she was naturally made chairman, and to appoint a treasurer to take charge of any money that might come in.

Within two years her organization had become a significant factor in the local political scene. In those days one of the best ways of reaching people from the country districts on any issue was to catch their attention at the state and county fairs, and in 1911, and again in 1912, she arranged to have booths set up in all of these to dispense free literature, posters and insignia touching on the suffrage question. Thus she had her organization, directed by the central committee; she had aroused interest in the public by her speech in the Montana legislature, and had kept that interest alive by her publicity campaigns. The situation began to look promising.

How effective all this was can be deduced from the fact that one prominent political figure after another came out for suffrage. The successful candidate for governor in November 1912, a Democrat named Samuel V. Stewart, pledged himself to support an equal-franchise amendment to the state constitution; many candidates for the legislature followed suit. True to his pledge, Governor Stewart in his inaugural address in January 1913 called on the legislature to act promptly on his recommendation, and as the session began, representatives who had only recently considered woman suffrage a great joke, if they had given it any thought at all, vied with one another for the privilege of introducing the measure. It seemed certain of passage, but Jeannette took no chances: besides urging her followers to bombard the members with letters, she herself interviewed every legislator personally and sat on the floor of the Chamber beside a supporter during the debate. The resolution to submit the amendment to the voters of the state was passed, with only two members dissenting, and was signed by the governor on January 25, almost a record for the course.*

So far so good, but there remained the problem of winning over a majority of the voters for the amendment. According to the Montana constitution, a proposed amendment needed mellowing: it could be submitted to the electorate only in the year following passage in the legislature, that is, in 1914. This gave the Montana Equal Franchise Society ample time to marshal its forces as well as to allow Jeannette to barnstorm around the rest of the country for the national association. At the beginning of 1914, however, she returned to Montana to direct the campaign. Headquarters were established in Butte, the state's richest city, whence letters were sent out to labor unions, granges and women's clubs asking for cooperation; instructions to local and county aides poured out in a steady stream; voters in the country districts were approached by mail, while in the cities suffrage workers made a house-to-house canvass. Leading suffragists, including Dr. Anna Howard Shaw, president of the national association, and Harriet Laidlaw, head of the New York Suffrage Party, came out to address meetings in many districts.

In the towns women spoke in motion picture theaters, or from wagons or automobiles, wherever they could muster up an audience, however small. The state was so large and its mountains made communication so difficult that campaigning in the rural areas was arduous. There the usual program was to hold a rally and then sweeten it with a dance on Saturday nights. Jeannette and her aides, one contemporary account tells, went into every little mining camp and settlement that could be reached. From the steps of little country stores they would address a group composed entirely of men, who listened in respectful silence, too shy to ask questions but ready to give the speakers

* Burton K. Wheeler, then a state representative (later United States Senator), tried at the last moment to relieve the solemnity of the occasion with a bit of buffoonery. With the connivance of his friend Pat O'Hern, who was then presiding, he rose to offer an amendment to the amendment: to the effect that only women with six children be granted the franchise. With equal solemnity, O'Hern declared him out of order.

a hand at the end of the talk. Old prospectors said: "Do you ladies really want to vote? Well, if you do, we'll sure help all we can." Horny-handed settlers also felt the force of the argument. "What would our state have been without the women?" they asked. "You can count on us."

As grand strategist Jeannette was "in and out of Butte, and in fact all over the state," it was reported in the *Woman's Journal,* the suffrage weekly, which also quoted what one voter had remarked about Jeannette: ". . . if she could talk personally to every voter in the state there would be no doubt of suffrage carrying, so great is her charm and so convincing her arguments." During one twenty-five-day period at this time she traveled 1,300 miles, giving a speech every day. Her method of campaigning in fact prefigures the political methods of today, by which a candidate using planes and helicopters and fast automobiles tries to meet, shake hands with or be seen by as many individual voters as possible, in shopping centers, at factory gates, or in the street. But whereas today such appearances are perfunctory, Jeannette's approach was direct, personal. She did address meetings, but she did not rely on them, as was customary in her time, for she was engaged in building a constituency from the ground up.

Optimistic though she was in regard to the outcome, she did not deceive herself about the size and strength of the opposition. One intimation of this came at the beginning of the year, when an antisuffrage representative came to Butte to consult with the liquor interests on how to stem the growing tide favorable to the women's party. This organizer urged the editor of *The National Forum,* a periodical put out by the association of saloon keepers, to tone down his opposition to the suffrage amendment because too obvious a tie between the liquor people and the antisuffragists would only backfire! (It was true that the Women's Christian Temperance Union, while indifferent to women's larger aims, favored granting votes to women because they foresaw that women would help them put over a Prohibition law.)

Jeannette turned the visit of the antisuffragist to good account, charging in a newspaper interview that the liquor interests were giving the antis financial backing. The antis, she said, "always have lots of money. We are frank to admit that we haven't much money, but we are always willing to publish details of our finances, which the opposition is not." There was also an attempt made to organize an antisuffrage society in the state, but it aroused little interest and gained few followers. Nevertheless, a Mrs. Oliphant came forward to challenge Jeannette to a debate in Helena, where for the first time that seasoned campaigner met a hostile audience. At a meeting packed with tough characters, every statement made by Mrs. Oliphant was wildly applauded, while Jeannette's voice could scarcely be heard above the jeers and gibes of the crowd.

The opposition was not limited to the liquor interests. Fearful that women voters would bring about passage of a workmen's compensation law, the great copper companies also worked more or less underground to block the amendment. The miners were not left in the dark as to how they were expected to vote.* After all, the issue of votes for women was to be decided by men, and it was difficult to tell whether the majority of men in Montana cherished their liquor more than women's rights, or were willing to risk their jobs for a principle.

Because of the large amounts of money at the command of the opposition, the suffragists were obliged to manage their limited funds thriftily. None of them received any pay, but still there were expenses for travel, for printing and mailing weekly bulletins to the newspapers, for paper and stamps for the innumerable letters addressed to the electorate. The needed money was raised the way women have always raised sums for local projects: through donations, food sales, dances, collections, and the sale of suffrage newspapers. One week was designated as "self-denial week," during which sympathizers pledged themselves to donate the money they saved by foregoing all luxuries such as theaters, afternoon teas, or movies. Almost on the eve of Election Day the bank in which all the campaign funds were deposited failed, but the national association and friends outside the state made up for the loss. The whole campaign cost only $9,000.

* In some company towns in Montana, it was reported later, the company let it be known that if their candidate did not win an election, every man in the locality would lose his job.

The suffragists never slackened their efforts right up to the end. It was decided to highlight the campaign with a parade at the opening of the state fair in Helena on September 25. Led by Anna Howard Shaw, Dr. Maria Dean (a leading woman doctor in Montana), and Jeannette, thousands of women and, it was said, as many men, stepped out smartly to the rhythm of several brass bands. An American flag was carried by representatives of states where full suffrage had been won; there were yellow flags for states where suffrage campaigns were in progress; gray banners for states with partial suffrage; and black banners for nonsuffrage states. The Indian girl Sacagawea was again represented. Unlike the Washington parade of the preceding year, this well-organized demonstration went off without a hitch and was warmly received by the crowds of visitors attending the fair. Children were offered sashes bearing the words: "I want my mother to vote"; suffrage booths were conspicuous; and *The Suffrage Daily* was hawked about the fairgrounds.

On Election Day, November 3, Jeannette gave further proof of her growing political expertise. To forestall the devious methods of party bosses, she made sure that there were poll-watchers on hand in all the city precincts to prevent the stuffing of ballot boxes. As the day wore on, the returns seemed to be fluctuating; in some counties the ballots were sealed up without a count. Suspecting fraud in Anaconda, a company town, Jeannette sent delegations of women there and enlisted the aid of local attorneys to prevent any tampering with the returns. It was not until the middle of November that the outcome was definitely known; suffrage carried by 44,302 in favor to 37,588 against.

At the very time the count was being checked the National American Woman's Suffrage Association was holding its annual convention in Nashville, Tennessee, but Jeannette sent word that she would not attend unless women won the vote in Montana. The news of her triumph preceded her appearance, and when at last she came before the assembled delegates she received a tumultuous welcome. She stood on the platform along with many other women who had devoted their lives not only to suffrage but to other humane causes as well. Among them, significantly, were Jane Addams, who had worked for the relief of the urban poor during a quarter of a century, and who was to spend her remaining years working for peace; and Rosika Schwimmer, feminist and pacifist from Hungary, who two years later was to induce Henry Ford to send his Peace Ship to Europe in an effort to end World War I.

Yes, suffrage had been won in Montana, and in the view of its advocates would soon be adopted all over the country. Despite her euphoria over the victory, however, Jeannette was aware that an even graver problem had arisen. In August 1914, while she was busy plotting the strategy to achieve the Montana victory, war broke out in Europe, and though its dark shadow did not yet reach the American continent, she was deeply troubled by the realization that nothing in her education or experience had prepared her for this.

IV

On Her Way

The pioneer strain, the drive to explore new territories and build up new settlements, was strong in Jeannette Rankin, a legacy from her venturesome parents. Like a pioneer or an artist she did not fear innovation or improvisation but rather courted them, in defiance of the caveats of either friends or critics. It had taken her eight years after her graduation from college to discover where her ruling interest lay, and now she was prepared to strike out into a field where no woman had trod before. The suffrage campaigns in which she had participated, particularly the one that led to victory in Montana, had revealed her qualifications for the art of democratic politics. There remained much work to be done for the suffrage movement, but the tide was clearly moving in its favor, so why should she not go forward, she asked herself, and win equality for women in a more advanced position?

The triumph of the suffragists in Montana was her creation. In the Washington and California campaigns she had played a minor role; in Montana she was the driving force. She had been the first to see the opportunity; she was the chief propagandist, the leading organizer, the architect of the victory. And the victory had been won by the use of those democratic methods in which she fervently and perhaps naïvely believed all her life, for despite many disappointments she always attributed her failures to imperfections in the machinery of the democratic process, not to democracy itself. During the suffrage campaign in Montana she had observed how people responded to a rational appeal for a good cause; moreover, she could not have failed to perceive that her own power to win adherents was a rare gift.

What, then, should be her next step? Clearly, since women could now vote in Montana, they could also be represented by a woman in Congress. The unfinished business with regard to suffrage in the rest of the country would be concluded more rapidly if a woman were to speak for women on Capitol Hill. And what woman was better qualified for this than Jeannette Rankin, whose name was on the lips of every voter, male and female, in the state; a candidate with a ready-made constituency?

Two years were to pass before Jeannette was to announce her candidacy, but the idea could not have been far from her mind once the cheers and the shouting died down in November 1914. Meanwhile, for the moment, she continued her work as field secretary of the national association into the spring of the following year; her travels took her to Washington once more, thence to New Hampshire, and from there to western Pennsylvania. As the summer came on, she resigned her post and went back to Missoula to lecture at the university summer school.

Her work in the suffrage movement meanwhile had not been so absorbing that she was able to put the war in Europe out of mind; for her, as for Jane Addams and many other suffrage advocates, the idea of a world without wars seemed naturally linked to the extension of the ballot to women. A Women's Peace Party had been founded as early as January 1915. It had sent Jane Addams, Emily Greene Balch and other delegates to an international meeting of women at the Hague to discuss what measures could be taken to stop the war before it became the graveyard of a whole generation. As a result of this meeting Jane Addams and Dr. Aletta Jacobs of Holland were deputed to visit the foreign offices of the warring powers to urge acceptance of mediation; Emily Balch was sent to Scandinavia and to Russia. The women were coldly received in the chancellories, a shade less so in Germany than by the Allies, but in both camps

Jane Addams, after a portrait by George de Forest Brush.

The New York Public Library

they were given to understand that peace without victory was unacceptable.

Jeannette had attended the meetings leading to the formation of the Women's Peace Party, and also served on the executive committee of a group of peace workers in New York at the Nurses Settlement (headed by Lillian Wald and later known as the Henry Street Settlement) who set themselves the task of working out peace proposals. Whatever her contribution to this project, it is obvious that she was beginning to give the question of peace some serious thought, even to entertain the notion that peace might be an attainable goal.

Meanwhile a short vacation after her university lectures in Missoula left her a bit restless—she had always found it difficult to damp down her engines—and in the fall of the year she decided to go abroad. But where could she go? Europe was out of the question because of the war, and the Orient presented too many difficulties of language and custom. In the end she chose to go to New Zealand for her holiday, influenced in part by the social progress in that faraway land where woman suffrage had been won as early as 1893! Another factor in her decision was her lean purse: with little money above her fare she would need to find a job, which was more likely in an English-speaking country. And intuitively she knew that a job would put her in a way to learn far more about the people than if she traveled as a mere tourist.

She embarked at Seattle for her first journey by sea and her first trip out of the United States. In New Zealand her skill with the needle stood her in good stead, for she quickly found work as a seamstress. Like other offshoots of British colonialism, New Zealand, she discovered, clung to the old hierarchical order: the owner of the dressmaking shop where she was employed ate lunch in the office, apart from her assistants. Jeannette stitched away quietly during working hours, but at lunchtime she engaged her fellow workers in conversation so interesting that the proprietor felt left out of things. She therefore asked Jeannette to seat herself near the door adjoining the office so that she could hear the discussion without breaking the social barrier.

Jeannette boarded at a "Girls' Friendly," a cooperative home, where after a short time she began prodding the other seamstresses to demand higher pay. At length she herself refused to accept the standard wage of six shillings and placed an advertisement in the local newspaper announcing that an American dressmaker would go out by the day for twelve shillings. Soon she had all the work she could handle, not, as she said later, because she was so expert, but for the reason that as an American she was expected to supply a certain chic the New Zealand women sadly lacked. In describing this experience later, Jeannette said, "I had forgotten what I did know about sewing by this time. If I made a mistake or forgot something, I'd say we would call it something else in America." She worked just long enough to pay for her food and lodging.

Wherever she went throughout her mature life, Jeannette seized the opportunity to talk to people, on the street, on a ship or train or plane. People were her raw material, her stock in trade. During her stay in New Zealand a dock strike took place, although strikes at that time were outlawed. Curious about this, particularly in a country that was otherwise rated as highly progressive, she went down to the waterfront and engaged the longshoremen in conversation. One of their leaders, a Scotsman named Fraser, proved to be especially articulate, though he had lost all his teeth, and impressed her as very intelligent despite his rough exterior. Many years later, when she was serving her second term in Congress, she read that the Prime Minister of New Zealand, Peter Fraser, was to appear before a House committee in Washington. She wrote him a note, asking if he remembered her and suggesting that they meet. His response was cordial, and though their meeting was brief, she was gratified to see that along with other signs of polish he had acquired an elegant set of dentures.

The New Zealand trip gave Jeannette a much-needed change and rest but, even more important, offered an occasion for self-appraisal and reflection which she had not enjoyed for about five years. Reviewing the suffrage campaigns, particularly the one in Montana, she realized that they had drawn on all her resources, all her initiative. And what was a suffrage campaign if not a political exercise? It required the same maneuvering, the same knowledge of legal possibilities, the same approach to the man and woman in the street. If she could run a successful suffrage campaign, there was no reason why she could not run for office, using the same techniques she had mastered in previous battles at the polls.

When she returned to Montana from New Zealand she had probably made up her mind to take the great leap forward and show that women could govern as well as vote. But the matter needed a tactful approach if she was not to alienate those who had given her such staunch support in the suffrage fight.* Before going abroad she had been instrumental in forming "good government clubs" all over the state to press for political and social reforms. In 1915 these clubs had mustered enough strength to win passage of mothers' pensions and equal guardianship laws,

* Up to very recently women have in the main shrunk from standing for office unless they were offered a place as the widow of a former officeholder. It has not been considered "ladylike" or "womanly" to be so forward. Men on the other hand are not so inhibited, and no one misesteems them when they announce their candidacy for the highest office in the land. It is only recently that women have broken through this barrier, as when Rose Bowman, running for the United States Senate in Idaho in the 1972 primaries, said that women had no right to grumble about having so small a share of seats in legislatures and the Congress. ". . . unless we put ourselves in the positions to be elected. . . . The only way we'll get there is to assert ourselves and have the confidence that we can do it."

thus proving that they had not lost the momentum of the equal franchise struggle. It was known, too, that many members of these clubs wished to test women's political maturity by electing one of their sex to office, beginning with some minor post.

A minor post did not, however, measure up to Jeannette's ambitions, which she broached to Wellington. Wellington said: Why not? Still, he advised her not to make her intention public before obtaining the approval of those who had been most active in the suffrage fight. At his suggestion she brought together a group of prominent women from all over the state to inquire whether they would support her if she decided to run for a seat in Congress. They were aghast at such presumption; they did want a woman in some elective office, to be sure, but urged that they aim for something less conspicuous than the United States Congress—a seat in the state legislature, for example—and not run the risk of an outstanding failure. Jeannette thought otherwise, and so did Wellington, who offered to look into the reaction of other groups to her candidacy. The reaction of party professionals was negative, as might have been expected, one prominent Republican advising that Wellington "keep Jeannette from making a fool of herself."

Indeed, aside from her daring to run for an office never before held by a woman, Jeannette betrayed a quixotic streak by venturing into politics in Montana, of all places. For many years Montana had been notorious throughout the country for the most flagrantly corrupt political practices. While she was growing up, the state had been the scene of ruthless exploitation by as picturesque and unprincipled a set of robber barons as this country has seen, their prize being control of the richest vein of copper then known to exist anywhere in the world. Though they were constantly feuding among themselves for financial gain, they joined forces to assert complete political authority in the state. This hegemony continued and was reinforced when the rival mining interests, at the beginning of the twentieth century, were consolidated into one giant corporation—the Anaconda Copper Company—always respectfully and often fearfully referred to as "the Company."

For the most part, however, the copper barons chose not to hold political office, preferring to operate through their kept political hirelings. The one exception to this rule was William Andrews Clark, who, after acquiring a vast fortune through astute manipulations, decided to crown his life's work by winning a seat in the United States Senate. This desire was so compelling that he spent half a million dollars to buy the honor, and succeeded only after having been rebuffed or outbid three times. He "made it" at last in 1900 and remained in the Senate for a full six-year term, without once opening his mouth in debate.

The Company meanwhile continued to dominate political activities in Montana without challenge, and a candidate like Jeannette, unproven by their standards, was not to their liking.

Taking other factors into consideration, however, Wellington became convinced that his sister could win election hands down. For one thing, with the exception of the governor himself, she was the best known person in the whole state, and for another, as he told an interviewer many years later, she was "the best single-handed campaigner" he had seen in all his years of politicking. As he foresaw, unlike the fainthearted suffragists whose advice she had originally sought, a majority of the women in Montana quickly rallied to her support, regardless of party affiliation, because they anticipated that the election of a woman to Congress would dramatize and probably expedite the passage of a national constitutional amendment for equal franchise.

With the encouragement of Wellington, who became her campaign manager, she therefore announced her candidacy early in July 1916 by filing a petition to run for a seat in the House of Representatives in the Republican Party primaries. There was no question as to what banner she would run under; her father had been a Republican, and Wellington, though he had bolted the party in 1912 to support Teddy Roosevelt and the Progressive Party, was now safely back among the regulars. Jeannette herself was fairly indifferent to party labels. When someone asked her many years later if she was a Republican at heart she replied: "I never was a Republican. I ran on the Republican ticket."

Seven men in addition to Jeannette entered their names for the nomination, and of this field of eight the two winning the highest number of votes would run on the party ticket against two Democratic candidates in November. Contrary to the expectations of the party leaders, Jeannette won this first engagement easily, coming out with 22,549 votes, against 15,439 for the nearest contender. Her vote was swollen by the support of many Democratic women, as for example that of Mrs. John Holt, the biggest cattle owner in eastern Montana, who gladly crossed party lines in order to help send a woman representative to Washington.

Now girding herself for the election campaign, Jeannette repeated the tactics that had been so effective in the suffrage battle. It should be pointed out that at this period the population of Montana was so small that the state was not divided into congressional districts but was represented by two congressmen-at-large. This meant that every city, town and hamlet in a vast area had to be covered, just as in 1914. On the other hand, it relieved her of the necessity of addressing herself to purely parochial issues, which would have been inevitable in a smaller district. The idea of congressmen-at-large, rather than congressmen representing limited districts (which are so susceptible to partisan gerrymandering), had always struck her as more democratic and in recent years came to be a program on which she spent much of her time and powers of persuasion.

Her platform in 1916, that is to say her personal platform, differed in some respects from that of the Republican Party, whose pious generalizations needed no lip service from her. She called for an amendment to the Federal Constitution to give women the vote, stronger legislation for the protection of children, and a radical revision of congressional rules to allow for the speedier passage of important legislation. In her published platform there was a plank on Prohibition, which she supported without stressing it in her speeches; she later confessed that she got little help from the Women's Christian Temperance Union in her campaign. An issue much closer to her heart was the war issue, and while her platform called for "preparedness for peace," she frequently stated her firm commitment to keep the United States out of the war in Europe. In that season Woodrow Wilson too, running for reelection as president, tried to find favor in the eyes of his countrymen by claiming that he had "kept us out of war."

The larger part of Jeannette's campaigning had a more intimate character than the public hall and the prepared speech in the larger cities. Unlike her Democratic opponents, or her running mate in the Republican Party, who, as she said, had "too much dignity" to seek out their constituents, she spoke from street corners or in lumbering camps; she went into homes to speak to women in their kitchens, and met men at the gates of the mines and smelters when they changed shifts. She once described to a friend her technique of electioneering in union halls:

> I would go into a union hall when they were having a meeting and ask to be allowed to speak for five minutes when they had concluded their business. Sometimes I would have to wait for an hour until they had finished, sitting in a corner without opening my mouth. When the chairman finally gave me leave to address the men, I found they listened with great courtesy and interest to what I had to say.

She covered large areas of the state, not, as John F. Kennedy wrote long afterward, on horseback, which would have been a truly Amazonian feat considering the distances to be traversed, but by automobile and train. When traveling by car she drove herself, not wishing to be known as an incompetent creature who needed a chauffeur to take her about. Whenever possible she went from place to place by train, a far more reliable service than it is today, and boasted later that on one trip she went 400 miles over the Rockies in an electric train—a great novelty in those days and one that was expected to revolutionize the railroad industry. Where she herself could not go, there went legions of her loyal supporters, not least of whom were her redoubtable sisters, Harriet, Mary, Grace and Edna. From Helena, Wellington kept track of public sentiment everywhere and warned her of traps laid by Republican machine politicians. On one occasion, when she hit the trail in company with her running mate, Wellington reported that her colleague, while pretending to support her on their joint appearances, would afterwards go into the local bars and crack jokes at her expense. On the whole she got little help from the party organization.

The most significant opposition she had to face came from the Anaconda Copper Company. The Company was accustomed to having elected officials who knew who was master in Montana, but the Rankins did not fit into that category. Wellington had built up a thriving law practice by serving as counsel to clients who resisted the Company in the courts, and Jeannette was correctly suspected of sympathy for the labor unions. As in the suffrage campaign, the Company made common cause with the liquor interests, which, along with the Company, controlled most of the newspapers in the state. Hence her campaign won a minimum of coverage, no paper giving any space at all to her statements against our entry into the war in Europe. Considering this powerful if covert opposition, her growing strength as the campaign drew to a close was somewhat mystifying to the political professionals.

Nationwide the newspaper coverage was not much better. It was not until early in November that the *Times* and the *Sun* in New York commented on the Montana contest, admitting the possibility that a woman might be elected to Congress. In the view of the editors of the *Times*, however, the possibility was extremely remote, for when Belle Fligelman, one of Jeannette's aides in Helena, sent them biographical material to be used in their postelection survey, it was returned to her without comment. As Election Day approached, the old guard in the Montana GOP came to understand that Jeannette might win, but they viewed the eventuality without undue alarm, for these seasoned manipulators had enough experience in handling elections to feel confident that if worse came to worst they could always bow to the election of a Democrat.

On November 6, 1916, Jeannette voted for the first time, since she had been in New Zealand the previous year. Then the waiting began. In the sudden quiet and suspension of activity the time passed with agonizing languor, for the tally could not begin until the polls closed, and the votes were then counted by hand. Late that night, unable to bear the suspense, she phoned the local newspaper in Missoula to learn the results thus far, trying to conceal her identity, as she told a friend, by inquiring first about the other candidates. "How did Wilson come out?" she asked. And after a few other queries: "How did Jeannette Rankin run?" "Oh, she lost," was the reply. It was with this disheartening news that she went to bed.

Next morning the gloomy forecast was confirmed by the Montana newspapers. Before the end of that day, however, her spirits were raised a little by more cheering intelligence. Wellington called her from Helena to report that her defeat was not certain by any means, that his analysis of the voting pattern in the counties indicated the contrary. Visitors to the house in Missoula, arriving to commiserate with her, were received with an air of "doubtful joy," as she described her feelings later. That afternoon there came a telegram from the *New York Times* asking how she stood, and on the basis of Wellington's findings she answered claiming victory. The Montana newspapers continued to deny this in their Thursday issues, and it was not until late on Friday evening that they conceded her election, by 7,567 votes.

She was the only Republican running for an important office to be elected in Montana that year; the Democrats won the other seat in Congress, the United States senatorship, the governorship, and other ranking posts, as well as giving Wilson a plurality of more than 34,000. Jeannette immediately attributed her victory to the women of Montana, who were determined, as she said at the time, "to have a woman represent their interest in Congress." Later she was to maintain that her success was due in equal measure to her stand against United States involvement in the war in Europe. And on many occasions afterward, she contended that those two significant factors would have been insufficient had it not been for the law that enabled her to run as congressman-at-large, thus winning votes from all over the state.

The three days of tension while waiting for the final tabulation of the ballots had been a great strain for Jeannette and for her family. Habituated as she was to action—a long-distance runner, in fact—she had found the idleness and the uncertainty almost unbearable. But this trauma was as nothing compared to what she was obliged to undergo once her victory was assured. The first woman elected to Congress! The first woman elected to any national representative body in the world! She was a phenomenon, a bombshell; she was news!

The whole world wanted to know all about her. What did she look like? Was she a woman or a freak? Could she cook? What did she think of current fashions? And to keep the world informed about these momentous matters journalists, magazine writers, photographers, and the merely curious besieged the big house on Madison Street relentlessly. She was asked to sponsor products of various kinds for a fee, or merely for a gift of the products themselves. Proposals of marriage came through the mails, one man writing that she was his "pan of milk and honey." Items about her election were published all over the globe, and one European journal aroused much indignation locally by describing Montana as bordering on Canada, when everyone knew that Canada bordered on Montana!

Friends and aides also appeared at her door, where the bell was rung continually by messengers with telegrams from all over the country and abroad. If she or members of her family showed some reluctance about divulging the desired information, no matter; slight acquaintances were invited to tell all they knew, or fancied they knew, about her habits, her character, and her life story. Jeannette was in a state of shock, she told a friend later, to find herself the object of such unsparing public interest. "It was very hard for me to comprehend . . . that it made a difference what I did do and didn't do from then on," she said. After about a week of living in a goldfish bowl she resolved to defend her privacy; she announced that she would not leave her home until all cameramen had left the premises, and this ban on photographers was not to be lifted until after the first of the year, when some of the excitement died down. She made only one exception to this: on November 17 she permitted a newsreel photographer to film her brief appearance before the student body of the University of Montana.

Apart from this one occasion she went into seclusion, refusing all social engagements and submitting to few interviews. She did receive a reporter from the *New York Times*, who quoted her in an article that reflected her somber mood and the degree of her engagement. "I feel a tremendous responsibility," she told him. "As Representative of the state of Montana, I shall represent to the best of my ability the men, women and children of my state. But in a certain sense I feel that it is my special duty to express also the point of view of women and to make clear that the women of the country are coming to a full realization of the fact that Congress is a body which deals with their problems."

Regardless of her sex, she was unusually well equipped for a seat in Congress, far more than most of the freshman congressmen being sent to Washington at that time. She was better educated than many of them, for one thing, and thanks to her years in the suffrage movement she had more than book knowledge of legislative practices. In the course of her extensive lobbying activities in state and national legislatures she had been obliged to learn parliamentary rules and the means by which bills are introduced and brought to debate; she knew the role of committees, which could further or modify or by inaction strangle a bill; she knew too the kinds of pressure that could be exerted by vested interests, and the loyalties exacted of party regulars.

She was thirty-six years old, a mature person, full of vigor and inured to hard work. There was work to be done in Congress, and she meant to take an active part in it, not be content to pose as a symbol or take a back seat on the pretext that she did not know the ropes. No longer shy or reserved after years in public life, she had manners so unaffected and winning that they concealed an iron core of resolution from all but her intimates. Her friendly gray-green eyes, her controlled voice, her style of dress were far from the popular conception of the militant suffragist, who was more often pictured as noisy, defiant, masculine; but those who thought she could be influenced to act against her better judgment were yet to learn the mettle of this staunch feminist and humanitarian.

V

"I Cannot Vote for War"

During the months between her election and her installation as a member of Congress, the beguiling flattery of public attention engaged Jeannette only peripherally; more vexing was the question of how she was to conduct herself after she was seated, what image she was to project as a woman where no woman had played a role before. Her principal concerns had been stated repeatedly during the campaign just ended: suffrage, the protection of children, social justice, the extension of democracy; and she had a general notion of the mechanics involved in getting such reforms as she advocated onto the statute books. A graver problem, however, was coming into the public consciousness in the winter of 1916–17, the matter of American involvement in the war in Europe, which she sensed would overshadow all other issues, perhaps efface them.

When the war broke out in Europe in August 1914 she was in the midst of the suffrage campaign in Montana, on an uninterrupted schedule of organizing, traveling, speaking, only dimly aware of what was going on in any other part of the planet. And yet on learning of the outbreak of hostilities, she felt as if the bottom of the world had fallen out, and it needed a tremendous effort for her to return to the business in hand. In the fall of 1916, while campaigning for Congress, she sensed the hot breath of war coming closer to our shores, and declared herself unequivocally opposed to American involvement in European quarrels. But now that she was a regularly elected member of Congress, she asked herself whether duty required her to change her position.

The war in Europe had already brought about great changes in the United States within the space of two and a half years, during which the flagging economy, recovering only feebly from the great panic of 1907, had received a shot in the arm from war orders by all the contending nations. Industry in general—not merely the manufacture of munitions, but agriculture, mining, shipping, banking—all showed great gains; employment had risen; prosperity was not around the corner, it was right here. Businessmen drew no fine moral distinctions about which side was right and which wrong, selling impartially to all customers, provided they could pay. The balance began to swing in favor of the Entente, however, when a consortium of American bankers granted the British loans with which to finance their purchases. Propaganda from England and France as well as Germany flooded the country, each side accusing the other of unimaginable atrocities, most of which were later disproved, save for the atrocity of war itself. In the propaganda battle the Allied powers had the advantage in the skill and persuasiveness of their publicists, their air of dauntless courage in the face of a ruthless antagonist, in contrast with the ineptitude of their German counterparts. Even more significant in the swing toward the Entente was the administration's gradual acceptance of a theory of national policy first enunciated by Henry Adams, which held that the interests of England, France and the United States, the three great maritime countries forming "the Atlantic System," required that they stand together against any threats from continental rivals.

It was not so much the war of words that brought American involvement in the conflict closer; it was the war on the sea lanes. To keep American munitions and goods from reaching the Central Powers, the Allies established a blockade of all ports to which Germany had access. The Central Powers responded with a blockade of British and French ports, but since her surface navy was immobilized, Germany carried on her blockade by means of submarines, in which she was superior. Both warring groups stopped, searched and confiscated American ships or cargoes, while the American government sent futile notes of protest to London and Berlin, claiming freedom of the seas. In May 1915 a German submarine sank the British ocean liner *Lusitania*, which was carrying munitions as well as more than a thousand passengers and crew, among them many Americans, most of whom lost their lives.* This disaster aroused such horror that the Germans suspended the submarine campaign temporarily, but on January 31, 1917, the German Ambassador abruptly notified Washington that it was to be resumed. It was while Wilson and his advisers were conferring on what steps should be taken in response to this provocative act that Jeannette made ready to take her seat in the House of Representatives.

Secluded though she was in her home in Missoula, Jeannette was far from idle in the months after her election to Congress. If she had had nothing more to do than paste up her scrapbooks she would have been occupied for weeks, since the papers and magazines were filled with stories, articles and cartoons about her, many of them inaccurate, some of them mocking, and a few even challenging her right to the seat. Christopher Morley, who passed for a wit, went so far as to publish some lame doggerel on the subject of a woman in Congress:

> Her maiden speeches will be known
> For charm and grace of manner
> But who on earth will chaperone
> The member from Montana?

* In an article in *Life*, October 13, 1972, "Lusitania, a Great Liner with Too Many Secrets," Colin Simpson revealed that the ship's cargo contained very large quantities of highly explosive material not listed on its manifest when it left New York Harbor. He suggested also that the British Admiralty unconscionably did nothing to prevent its sinking or to rescue survivors. There is a definite implication that the catastrophe was courted in order to bring the United States into the war, in line with Winston Churchill's view that "the maneuver which brings an ally into the field is as serviceable as that which wins a great battle." For the moment the maneuver did not have the effect he desired, possibly because there was a great outcry in the United States about permitting munitions to be carried on a passenger vessel, even though the extent of the cargo was not then known.

Before she went East to what she rightly anticipated would be a busy schedule in the public eye, one matter she had to settle was her wardrobe. Although she liked to wear pretty hats, she did not customarily rely on striking headgear to establish her personality. Not for her the modest tricorne affected by Frances Perkins when she went to Washington as the first woman Cabinet member, or the dashing big-brimmed hats of Bella Abzug. Jeannette was clothes-conscious in a sophisticated way, insisting that whatever she wore should be well made, of fine materials, becoming and appropriate, with a perfect fit, so that she need give the problem no further thought—every woman's dream. Still she would scarcely have been able to afford elegant clothes had it not been for Wellington, who numbered among his clients a man who knew some of the best dressmakers in New York. Convinced by this man that Jeannette ought to be launched on her career handsomely dressed, Wellington offered to have her outfitted in the metropolis at his expense, although he himself had only begun to make his mark as a lawyer. Fortunately for both of them, she never cared for expensive jewelry or accessories, but still the outlay for apparel on her first appearance as a congresswoman came to a sum normally beyond her means.

For her means were definitely limited. Aside from her expenses, she had received no pay from the National American Woman Suffrage Association, and the income of $75 a month she drew from her father's estate did not go very far. As a figure of national prominence, however, she was now in a way to make more money than she had ever earned before, beyond her salary as a member of the House. This new source of revenue was the lecture platform, for then, as now, Americans willingly paid to see and hear anyone who made the headlines, whether for achievement or for some suggestion of scandal attached to them. There were those who did not quite know in which category Jeannette belonged. On Wellington's advice she signed a contract with the Lee Kedick lecture bureau—a highly reputable agency—to go on a speaking tour at the rate of $500 per lecture, a fantastic sum for one who had been speaking her mind for free on many a public platform for more than six years. Within a few weeks she was able to pocket $10,000.

Her speeches were not read from a text, but for that reason they had to be prepared with special care, and this preparation took up much of her time before she set out on her tour late in February 1917. A practiced public speaker, she always knew just what she wanted to say, and once she was able to break through her own reserve she needed help only in her delivery. A voice teacher in Missoula had given her some instruction in this, but more useful still was special training in breath control which she received during the California campaign, and a course in public speaking at the University of Washington.* She did not strive for dramatic effects, relying instead on a tone of earnestness and reason, addressing herself to the concerns of her audience and winning their sympathy with her unpretentious bearing.

Accompanied by Wellington, she arrived in New York City to begin her lecture tour on February 24, 1917, staying at the home of her friend Mrs. Laidlaw at 6 East 66th Street. Only the day before, President Wilson had called for an extraordinary session of Congress, and it was no secret that he intended to ask Congress for a declaration of war against Germany. The man described in later years by Erik Erikson, the psychologist, as "a moralist of deep neurotic bent," had come hesitantly, with many misgivings, to this decision, for the role he had hoped to play earlier in the war was that of peacemaker, negotiating between the hostile forces as a neutral, with nothing to gain from victory on either side. If he were to lead the nation into war he was certain to base his action on the highest possible moral ground, in defense of sacred rights and duties, in a crusade to destroy evil and win the world for virtue.

On Jeannette's arrival in New York, therefore, the newspapermen descended on her in force to pose the all-important question: How would she vote on a declaration of war? "I cannot say anything about that at this time," she answered. She also fended them off when they inquired about her views on universal military service. Her answer to this was a curious one; her atti-

* On the platform she employed almost no gestures, mindful of a story told her by Dr. Anna Howard Shaw. When Dr. Shaw studied at a theological seminary the men were taught to use the whole arm when making a point. "What should a woman do?" someone asked. The teacher pondered a moment, then replied: "Just use the forearm."

Harriet Laidlaw, New York suffrage leader, Miss Rankin's friend and sponsor in the suffrage movement.

The Bettmann Archive, Inc.

tude, she said, would "depend upon the question of the welfare of the child involved." If she was referring to the induction of youths under the age of twenty-one, this statement was consistent with her proposal during her campaign for Congress, one she was to restate again and again over the years, that only older men, those who made the decision to go to war, should be sent to fight, leaving the younger men at home to propagate the race.

A capacity audience attended her appearance at Carnegie Hall on March 2. Handsomely dressed in a white evening gown, she spoke without notes on the subject of "Democracy and Government." It was a fairly radical speech for the time, reflecting her views on the reform of American society within the framework of the democratic system, somewhat along the lines of Theodore Roosevelt's Progressive Party platform, but going further still in criticizing the economic and political structure of the country. Beginning with a description of Montana, its beauties, its riches, and its problems, she soon went on to matters of national concern, referring to the labor troubles at Ludlow, Colorado, where striking coal miners and their families had been subjected to a savage massacre by the Rockefeller-dominated mining companies in 1914. Broadening her charge to include other vested interests, she commented on existing industrial conditions throughout the country, "under which a few people own most of the resources in every state."

"We must have political democracy, business democracy, social democracy," she maintained. Votes for women represented only a first step in the extension of democracy to all phases of American life. Children, too, needed the protection of the law. Elected officials must be held responsible to all the people after election, as before. "I am in favor of the initiative, the referendum, the recall, the direct primary, state and national Prohibition, a popular vote for president and a system of proportional representation in state legislatures," she said. And in conclusion she broached the subject of greatest interest to her listeners that night: "Women," she claimed, "ought to have a right to say whether their men shall go to war."

With few modifications, due to changed conditions and some advances, what she said at Carnegie Hall was to remain her personal platform all her life, and much of her speech is as applicable today as it was then. It went far beyond the simple dogma of the suffrage party, indicating a grasp of issues that concerned all the people, and asserting her right to propose remedies for the nation's ills. She found the control of the economy by a few persons or corporations unacceptable. Granting the high wages of most industrial workers, she maintained that their wages always shrank in buying power as the cost of living went up. She was one of the earliest to call for the popular election of the president and for proportional representation in state legislatures. She asserted her belief, too, that if women were allowed to take part in decision-making, wars could be prevented. Her general thesis was that only through the extension of the democratic process could effective reforms be brought about in the body politic. Above all she gave notice that she would not be a passive member of Congress but would measure the usefulness of her vote there on any legislation against a philosophy of government that had been maturing in her mind for many years.

Her New York speech was only the first of about twenty

speaking engagements for which she had contracted in cities scattered throughout the Northeast and Middle West, all within the space of a little more than a month. The period was enlivened for her by two memorable encounters, one with a man on his way up in public esteem, and the other with one on his way down. When she arrived in New York she received an invitation to lunch with a young man who, like her, had just been elected to Congress on the Republican ticket for the first time: Fiorello LaGuardia. In speaking of this meeting Jeannette recalled LaGuardia's warm, comradely spirit, noting with justifiable pique that he was the only Republican congressman in New York at that time who took any note of her existence. LaGuardia proved to be a staunch friend both in the House and afterward and showed his respect for her in his oft-quoted remark: "This woman has more courage and packs a harder punch than a regiment of regular-line politicians."

The other encounter was with Theodore Roosevelt, that "Byronic cowboy," as one historian described him, who invited her and Wellington to dinner at Oyster Bay. Since Wellington had long been an uncritical admirer of Roosevelt, the invitation to meet the ex-president flattered and excited him; he spoke of it as "the most important engagement of my life." To ease their journey out to Sagamore Hill, Mrs. Laidlaw, Jeannette's hostess, offered her own car and chauffeur, and the Rankins drove off in state. Unfortunately the chauffeur lost his way among the welter of narrow roads on northern Long Island, and Wellington's exaltation turned to despair when he realized that they would be forty-five minutes late for dinner with his idol.

They need not have been uneasy, for Roosevelt at that period felt so neglected by his fellow citizens that he greeted every visitor with almost pathetic eagerness. He kept them there until midnight, pouring out his views and his gripes on every conceivable subject: the war in Europe and how it could have been stopped if "that fellow in the White House" had done what Roosevelt advised; what he thought of the Kaiser (not much); what he thought of Lincoln; the labor movement, and a dozen other topics, with frequent references to *his* days in the White House. The bitter man held the floor, with an occasional assist from Wellington, but Jeannette said little. Wellington had hoped that Roosevelt would urge Jeannette to vote for a declaration of war, but the subject never came up. Possibly Roosevelt thought such advice was supererogatory; moreover, it is doubtful that he sought Jeannette's opinion on anything. Later Jeannette commented drily on the discussion that evening: "I appreciated that he thought the situation in Europe required war, but he said nothing to me to indicate that he wanted to influence my vote."

For weeks before she took her seat in Congress, pressure had been building up on all sides to get her to declare herself, but she was too astute to announce her intentions beforehand. There was even a financial consideration at stake; her lecture contract—and one wonders how Wellington permitted this clause to be inserted—provided that it was to be terminated if she voted against the war resolution. This had less weight with her than any of the other arguments with which she was bombarded. She listened to everyone but kept her own counsel. Aside from her lecture engagements, she made two other appearances, one before a Connecticut constitutional committee and another before the New Jersey legislature to plead for suffrage amendments. On April 1 she went down to Washington to be installed as the member from Montana at the special session of the Sixty-fifth Congress.

In Washington she had rented an apartment at 2030 California Street, quarters large enough to house herself and her mother as well as two secretaries, Belle Fligelman and Florence Leach. (A few weeks later Jeannette's sister Harriet Sedman, whose husband had died the day Jeannette took office, came to Washington with her two little girls, and the two young secretaries moved out to make room for this addition to the family.) After a short stop at her new home Jeannette went on to her office on Capitol Hill, which she found lavishly decorated with flowers and crammed with well-wishers and the usual swarm of newspapermen.

Again the reporters clustered around like bees on a comb. How would she vote on the speakership? She would abide by the recommendation of the Republican party caucus. Would she then vote with the Republicans on all legislative matters? That would depend on the legislation involved. In general, she told them, she proposed to support all legislation furthering woman suffrage, child welfare, and Prohibition. And then came the cardinal question: How would she vote on the war resolution? Still patient, she said she preferred not to indicate what she intended to do in that regard, and no one could trap her into an admission. The reporters nevertheless continued to press close around her, peppering her with questions, while friends pushed forward to shake her hand and strangers clamored for autographs. At length she threw up her hands. "I'm flustered!" she cried, and asked that the room be cleared.

Such are the miseries of fame. The grandeurs were to be savored the next day, when she would take her place on the great stage in the halls of Congress. On the morning of April 2 she was the guest of honor at a breakfast in the Shoreham Hotel given by the National American Women Suffrage Association. Seated between Carrie Chapman Catt, president of the Association, and Alice Paul, leader of the newly established Woman's Party (formerly the Congressional Union), she could look down the table at the beaming faces of old friends and fellow workers and see that her triumph was theirs. It was the highest point thus far reached in the suffrage struggle, but it also marked the last moment in the united front of the women's movement, soon to be rent into factions that would not be reconciled for half a century. Mrs. Catt saw equal suffrage as the end goal, while Alice Paul viewed it merely as a step forward in women's liberation from all political and social restrictions.

On that glorious day, however, the cracks in the movement were papered over, for there sat Jeannette Rankin, symbol of what they had achieved by their joint efforts, and token of what they could do in the future. Even before she made her little speech of acknowledgment, however, Jeannette indicated that she meant to be more than merely a token representative in Congress. One concerned woman present that morning was Julia Lathrop, head of the Children's Bureau which had been set up in the Department of Labor during the Taft administration. Miss Lathrop had been frustrated in her attempts to interest congressmen in legislation for the protection of children; they gave her scant attention. Jeannette was more forthcoming. On meeting Miss Lathrop she did not wait for the bureau chief to

Jeannette Rankin speaking from the balcony of the National American Woman Suffrage Association headquarters in Washington, April 2, 1917, before proceeding to the Capitol to be installed as the first woman Member of Congress. Carrie Chapman Catt is standing behind her.

Montana Historical Society

call on her for assistance, but said at once: "What can I do to help?" (In the course of her first term she worked closely with Miss Lathrop in this area.)

Her remarks to the assembled guests were an appeal and an affirmation. "I want you to know," she said, as she had said often since her election, "how much I feel this responsibility. There will be many times when I shall make mistakes, and it means a great deal to me to know that I have your encouragement and support." Then she continued: "The day after election it looked very much as if I had not been elected, but it seemed to me that the campaign had been nevertheless worthwhile because the women had stood together, the women had learned solidarity. . . . That one thing had been alone worth striving for." In asking for their loyal support, it was as if she meant to prepare

Driving to the Capitol to take her seat in Congress.

United Press International Photo

them for actions she might take in the near future, actions with which not all of them would agree, but for which she craved their tolerance and understanding.

Following her speech she drove to the headquarters of the association, where she stepped out on the balcony to address a crowd that had gathered in the street outside. From there she proceeded to the Capitol in an open touring car filled with flowers.

She entered the House of Representatives for her first session in Congress carrying a sheaf of blossoms from the morning's festivities—no violets this time. Coming down the aisle on the arm of her elderly Montana colleague, John Evans, she was met with cheers and applause from Democrats as well as Republicans on the floor, echoed by proud relatives and friends in the gallery. Ellen Maury Slayden, wife of the Representative from Texas, sat in the gallery that day and set down her impressions of the first congresswoman in her diary. Not more than a year earlier, wrote Mrs. Slayden, men would say when arguing against woman suffrage, " 'Next thing you'll be wanting women in Congress,' as if that were the *reductio ad absurdum,* and here she was coming in." A sharp observer, if something of a snob, Mrs. Slayden described Jeannette as looking like "a mature bride rather than a strong-minded female."

> She wore a well-made dark blue silk and chiffon suit, with open neck, and wide white crepe collar and cuffs; her skirt was a modest walking length, and she walked well and unselfconsciously. . . . She didn't look to right or left until she reached her seat, . . . but before she could sit down she was surrounded by men shaking hands with her. I rejoiced to see that she met each one with a . . . frank smile and shook hands cordially and unaffectedly. It would have been sickening if she had smirked or giggled or been coquettish; worse still if she had been masculine and hail-fellowish. She was just a sensible young woman going about her business. When her name was called the House cheered and rose, so that she had to rise and bow . . . which she did with entire self-possession.*

A photograph taken at the time shows the member from Montana in the costume she wore on that occasion, her brown hair framing the upper part of her face but not shadowing the large, brilliant eyes, tilted down at the corners, the strong, straight nose, the generous mouth with its half-concealed (Mona Lisa?) smile, the somewhat stubborn set of the chin, in all a very personable young woman in any milieu. Her dress was in fact so becoming and appropriate that one congressman was heard to suggest that all women elected to Congress thereafter be required to adopt it.

This first meeting of the House in the special session of the Sixty-fifth Congress was purely formal, its only business to admit new members and choose a speaker. Since there was a Democratic majority, Champ Clark, as expected, won the gavel. Jeannette voted with the Republicans. The real business of the ses-

* The diarist's husband, Mr. Slayden, was among the first of his colleagues to speak to her, remarking later to his wife that "she was not pretty but had an intellectual face and a nice manner." Mrs. Slayden, quite a beauty herself, was not pleased with her husband's reference to Jeannette's mental attributes, and two years later, on meeting her at the home of Mrs. Louis Post, wrote in her diary: "Miss Rankin doesn't appall me with her intellectuality."

Jeannette Rankin in the costume she wore when she took her seat in Congress in April 1917.

Montana Historical Society

sion was to begin in the evening, when the Senate would meet jointly with the House to hear a message from the President of the United States. At a few minutes past eight-thirty Wilson appeared before them to read his speech calling for war with Germany.

It was an elegant piece of rhetoric, full of memorable phrases: "the right is more precious than peace"; "America is privileged to spend her blood and might for the principles that gave her birth"; and grandest and hollowest of all: "make the world safe for democracy," which was to inspire millions of men and women all over the globe before it lost its resonance in the irony of events. Wilson had a gift for using hackneyed expressions in a way that made them seem glamorous and newly minted, but even if his speech had been insipid it would have had the same result, for the war party was in the ascendant in the halls of Congress. He was greeted with respectful applause when he concluded, and the senators returned to their chamber, where a joint resolution calling for a declaration of war was presented and referred to the Foreign Relations Committee.

The next day but one, April 4, the Senate met again to debate the resolution, which had been favorably reported out of committee, before a full house and crowded galleries. It was the occasion for a flood of patriotic oratory in a pale imitation of Wilson's measured periods; words like "right" and "justice" and "freedom" punctuated every speech, along with many a tender reference to Old Glory. The Senate, however, was not unanimous. A few voices speaking in a less belligerent vein were also heard, among others those of Senators Vardaman, Norris, and particularly LaFollette. The Senator from Wisconsin charged that there was no difference between the depredations of the warring powers; that England as well as Germany had preyed on our shipping. Among the Allies we were being called on to join in defense of democracy, he continued, there was no less autocracy than in the Central Powers, as for example in Russia, or in England's dominion over Ireland, India and Egypt. His most telling argument, however, and the one that struck Jeannette most forcibly was that the American voters had never authorized their government to plunge the nation into war, and that if the question were put to a referendum, the government would be defeated ten to one. This type of rational discourse only incited the war party to greater fury as they denounced the dissidents for want of patriotism, calling them outright traitors. When the tally was taken, the resolution to go to war passed overwhelmingly: 82 in favor, 6 against, and 8 not voting.

The House met on Thursday, April 5, and as at the Senate, the debate was followed closely by crowds packing the galleries and milling through the corridors and offices of the Capitol. Although the outcome was never in doubt, interest centered on how certain congressmen would vote, and particularly on Jeannette, as the first woman representative. It seemed to many suffragists and their sympathizers that the whole issue of woman suffrage and the right of women to hold office would be undermined if she took the unpopular side. Wellington was already committed to America's entrance into the war on the side of the Allies, and tried to convince her of the justice of that position, but beyond this he urged her to vote aye because a nay vote would end her career in politics. He wanted her to vote "a man's vote." "I knew she couldn't be elected again if she did vote against the war," he said later. "I didn't want to see her destroy herself."

Miss Rankin's office at the Capitol during her first term. Miss Rankin is seated far right, her sister Harriet Sedman next left.

Montana Historical Society

But not for nothing did Jeannette have that stubborn set of chin. Her answer to such reasoning was: "Never for one second could I face the idea that I would send young men to be killed for no other reason than to save my seat in Congress." Even less could the loss of income from her lecture contract play any part in her thinking. Still she gave Wellington to understand that she had not yet definitely made up her mind. In desperation he resorted to one last means of persuasion: he induced Mrs. Laidlaw to come to Washington to plead with Jeannette on behalf of the suffrage cause. Along with others among Jeannette's old associates, Mrs. Laidlaw thought that suffrage would sustain an irreversible setback if the congresswoman were to vote "irresponsibly," as some of them said. Having the matter put in this light was very painful for Jeannette. She told Mrs. Laidlaw that as of that moment she could not see her way to voting in favor of war, but she promised to listen carefully to the debate to be sure she had not overlooked any significant arguments, and said she would not cast her vote until the last moment. It had been made clear to her that unless she did as she was advised, she risked losing the love and respect of many of those dearest to her. The estrangement of old friends was not a matter to be lightly dismissed; still, it had to be weighed against her own self-respect. One had to be strong to be so much alone.

She listened scrupulously to the debate, as she had promised, but gained no new insights into the problem. Wrapped in the flag, one congressman after another rose to proclaim that love of country and engagement in the war were indivisible. A few dissenters warned of the loss of civil liberties that would follow a declaration of war; this had already been indicated by mobs breaking up antiwar meetings, and police bans on all so-called unpatriotic demonstrations; some, like LaFollette in the Senate earlier, warned of the grave implications of the espionage and conscription bills already drawn up, bills which the administration intended to push through Congress as soon as the war resolution was passed. Others who claimed that mail from their constituents was overwhelmingly opposed to the war were hissed and reviled as disloyal cowards, stooges of the Kaiser. (Jeannette's mail from Montana was running 16 to 1 against our involvement.) Only the sober remarks of Claude Kitchin of North Carolina, the majority leader, won any respectful attention, when he said: "It takes neither moral nor physical courage to declare a war for others to fight." Jeannette did not ask for the floor, an omission for which she was to reproach herself later, for some members told her after the vote was taken that they too would have voted for peace if they had known what stand she would take.

The debate began at ten o'clock in the morning and went on beyond midnight, which meant that the fateful decision would be made on Good Friday. Jeannette listened to most of the speeches but took refuge in her office during part of the evening to escape the highly charged atmosphere of the chamber, only to be subjected once more to Wellington's entreaties. When they were both exhausted he gave way. "Well," he said, "you've heard it all. You go in there and vote your conscience." She returned to the House for the first roll call.

"It was a different roll call," she remembered, "from any I had ever seen from the gallery. Every vote was watched with intensity. When they called my name there was a hush, and I didn't say a word." Some members attributed her silence to ignorance of the House rules, but from her experience as a lobbyist she knew that she need not vote until the second roll call. Uncle Joe Cannon, the veteran Republican leader and former Speaker of the House, threaded his way to her seat and offered some fatherly advice. "Little woman," he said, "you cannot afford not to vote. You represent the womanhood of the country in the American Congress. I shall not advise you how to vote, but you should vote one way or another—as your conscience dictates." Both Cannon and Wellington evidently hoped that her conscience in the end would lead her to the ethics of war.

The second roll call began. As the clerk read her name, the *New York Times* reporter wrote, all eyes in the galleries were turned on Miss Rankin. There was a breathless silence. She rose to her feet and involuntarily, as she recalled, made what proved to be the best speech of the debate, as well as the most succinct. "I want to stand by my country," she said, "but I cannot vote for war. I vote no." There was a thin flurry of applause from the gallery, and then the utmost confusion reigned. The new member had broken a precedent dating back 140 years, according to which no member was to remark on his vote during roll call. This was of no great moment, for Jeannette Rankin had broken a precedent of 140 years in being there at all. In commenting on her statement many years afterward, she said that if she had thought it out, she wouldn't have spoken in that way. "Under the circumstances, I didn't say it; it was said for me."

The story in the *New York Times* described her as being in a state bordering on frenzy, weeping copiously during the roll call, but witnesses who sat near her recalled that on the contrary she was dry-eyed and composed. "I had wept so much that week," she herself related, "that my tears were all gone by the time the vote came."*

Nor was she the only one to vote no on the war resolution, contrary to popular belief; the final tally was 374 for, 50 against, and 9 not voting. When the House adjourned at 3:14 A.M. on

* Clark Howell, editor of an independent paper in North Carolina, wrote the only editorial that condoned her tears, although under the misapprehension that she had wept during the roll call. "And why shouldn't Miss Rankin have cried?" he said, considering what she was being asked to do.

April 6, 1917, the nation was at war, lacking only the formal declaration by the President later in the day.

Long years afterward Jeannette remarked to a friend that none of the forty-nine men who voted with her were penalized as she was in consequence of her action. For almost immediately the superpatriots began their vilification of the lone woman representative. The Helena *Independent* said of her that she was "a dagger in the hands of the German propagandists, a dupe of the Kaiser, a member of the Hun army in the United States, and a crying schoolgirl." Ministers thundered that she was a disgrace to womanhood and that her behavior proved how inadequate women were for the demands of public office. Many suffragists also denounced her, charging that she had betrayed them. Carrie Chapman Catt, who had offered the entire National American Woman Suffrage Party for military service in case of war, wrote to a correspondent on April 8 in a tone of complete disillusionment: "Whatever she has done or will do is wrong to somebody, and every time she answers a roll call she loses us a million votes."

Alice Paul was one of the few suffragists who applauded her for putting women on record as opposed to war. Before the vote on the amendment was taken, Miss Paul and Hazel Hunkins of the Woman's Party went to see Jeannette to tell her that they couldn't publicly oppose the war *as an organization* because they wished to include all women who worked for equality for women; as individuals, however, they wanted to tell her that they thought it would be tragic if the first woman elected to Congress were to vote for war. They maintained that women were the peace-loving half of the world and that if power were given to women the possibilities of war would be diminished. Both suffragist leaders proved to be wrong in the long run, Mrs. Catt for saying that Jeannette's vote had put the suffrage amendment back "for years and years," and Alice Paul for claiming that votes for women would make wars less likely.

Of course it would have been much more agreeable for Jeannette and for the suffragists if there had been no soul-searching decision to be made immediately upon her entrance into Congress, or if she had gone along with the majority, without calling attention to herself and to her pacifist views. Her opponents among the suffragists thought it more important for her to build

Representative Jeannette Rankin planting a Montana fir tree on the Capitol grounds, Arbor Day, 1917. Belle Fligelman, her secretary, is on the left. The group includes two congressmen—Bacon of Michigan and Randall of California—Capitol officials, and women visitors.

up a reputation as a "responsible" legislator than to win "notoriety" on a matter of principle.

Jeannette did not share that view. As she reflected on the matter many years later, she said: "I believe that the first vote I cast was the most significant vote and a most significant act on the part of women, because women are going to have to stop war. I felt at the time that the first woman [in Congress] should take the first stand, that the first time the first woman had a chance to say no to war she should say it. That was what held me up with all the pressures being brought to get me to vote for war."

When she finally got to bed that morning Jeannette slept soundly. And when the storm broke over her head in the days that followed, she was not dismayed. She had betrayed no one; she had not been false to herself. Having gone through a formidable initiation as a member of Congress, she looked forward ardently to active participation in the affairs of the country.

VI

The Member from Montana

Soon after the United States declared war against Germany, Arthur Balfour, First Lord of the Admiralty in the Lloyd George government, arrived from London to confer with the President and other leading figures in the Wilson administration. In Balfour's honor a reception was to be held at the Willard Hotel, attended by the President, his cabinet, officials of high and low degree, and all the members of Congress. In due course Jeannette received an invitation. If she accepted, she would be the only woman present at the function, for wives were not included on such occasions, and it was generally assumed that she was too "ladylike" to appear as the only representative of her sex in a gathering of almost a thousand men. While she was debating the matter in her mind, a woman from Missouri who had been unsuccessful in trying to obtain an invitation for herself kept urging Jeannette to attend, if only to break down the barrier against all women at such affairs. The State Department, she told Jeannette, had informed her that the congresswoman was not expected. This was enough of an incentive for Jeannette; the State Department had no control over her movements.

As she passed down the room she was greeted by and soon completely surrounded by the other members of Congress as they learned she was present, all pressing forward to talk with her. At this point a voice was heard announcing "The President of the United States!" and at once the crowd around Jeannette parted, leaving a broad path open to the door of the room. There was nothing for Wilson to do then but to march down the cleared space to bid her welcome, before greeting the other guests, including Balfour. The first woman in Congress had broken yet another precedent.

When in the long file moving toward the receiving line she came face to face with Balfour, "the ruler of the Queen's navee" shrank back in dismay. Could this woman be the American counterpart of those militant English suffragettes who had not hesitated to commit acts of violence before the war? Pulling himself together quickly when he saw that she brandished no weapons or placards, he murmured something about not having expected to find a woman present. "I am a member of Congress," Jeannette said mildly, and moved on.*

This was not the only occasion on which Jeannette was obliged to use all her social graces to establish new patterns of behavior for women and overcome prejudice in what had been an exclusively male club for more than a century. Her own self-esteem precluded an apologetic or deferential attitude toward her colleagues; after all, she was an equal among equals, and for her own sake, as well as on behalf of the women who were to follow after her in public office, it was important that she act with assurance as well as dignity. She was the member from Montana and she intended to function in that role, not play the part of a fainthearted female who had strayed by chance into the councils of men. Thanks to her buoyant temperament, moreover, she was not intimidated or diverted from her objectives by the abuse to which she had been subjected because of her opposition to the war.

Nevertheless, she was realistic about the deeply ingrained male bias of some of her fellow congressmen and gave them no

* It was a matter of indifference to her whether she was called "Congressman," "Congresswoman," or "Member of Congress," although she probably preferred the last title. She did not share the view of liberationists that her sex had to be indicated in the way she was addressed, believing that the word or suffix "man" meant "human being" no less than "male."

opportunity to charge her with frivolity or triviality. On the whole she met with great courtesy. As often as possible she chose to sit next to an older man, white-haired, reserved, a newcomer to Congress like her, in order to refute any suggestion that she was a flirt. He for his part thoughtfully removed the ubiquitous spittoon from between their seats for her greater comfort. As many congressmen at that period, coming from rural districts, were habitual tobacco-chewers (the rest smoked cigars), this gesture must have represented a real sacrifice of his convenience. One Republican congressman, Joe Walsh of Massachusetts, was such an outspoken opponent of suffrage that she always made a point of taking a seat behind him so that the sight of her would not be a thorn in his flesh, as she put it.

In the main she was not made to feel like an interloper, as some of her fellow members were old acquaintances and treated her with easy camaraderie. Some felt friendly enough to advise her with respect to a congressman's first duty (to himself): to start the campaign for reelection immediately. Jeannette did not take advantage of this well-meant counsel, believing in all innocence that good conduct in office would be sufficient to guarantee the support of a majority of her constituents if she ran again.

There were other areas in which she sought and followed the advice of her colleagues. Despite her familiarity with many aspects of legislative procedure, she realized that every representative body had its peculiar customs, the accretion of long years, shaped to some degree by special situations or strong personalities of the past. She knew that she was green and would need direction to avoid mistakes that might impede the legislation she hoped to put through. It was this awareness that led her to invite two experienced members to lunch with her soon after her arrival in Washington—Evans of Montana and Gallivan of Massachusetts, two old hands who could be relied upon to steer her away from pitfalls.

Some aspects of her situation as the first woman in Congress were comical. She had known that she would be working in a man's world permeated by the fumes of tobacco and liquor, and she was prepared to cope with this. What was more uncomfortable was the lack of toilet facilities for women in the vicinity of the chamber. As it had seemed inconceivable that women would ever be elected to Congress, no provisions had been made for them, and Jeannette and her secretaries had to make their way through a maze of corridors and stairways to reach the public accommodations. Apropos of this she liked to tell a story about Dr. Mary Walker, who had obtained the right to wear men's clothing by act of Congress when she served as a doctor in the Civil War and who continued to appear in a frock coat, black broadcloth trousers and stovepipe hat for the rest of her life. Dr. Walker frequently turned up on Capitol Hill to lobby for one cause or another, to the terror of Jeannette's secretaries, who would come running from the ladies' room to wail that there was a man in the women's toilet! *

Jeannette's office staff consisted at first of Belle Fligelman and Florence Leach, two enthusiastic young women who had worked closely with her in Montana since the beginning of the 1914 suffrage campaign. Belle Fligelman (now Mrs. Norman Winestine) describes herself at that time as starry-eyed, confident that Jeannette was going to make a brave new world. Florence Leach left Washington after a few months, and her place was taken by Jeannette's sister Harriet, who assumed the management of the office, but Belle remained throughout the session, serving in many ways but particularly as Jeannette's literary secretary.** It was she who ghosted a weekly series of articles on topics of interest to women that appeared for about a year in the *Chicago Herald* and were widely syndicated under Jeannette's name. The staff was increased by the addition of a competent stenographer, since Jeannette's other assistants were indifferent typists and could not take dictation, as well as by a "department secretary" who handled all business between the constituents back home and the various Washington bureaus.

* One day a high wind blew up with such force that it knocked the old woman down on the steps of the Capitol, a fall that proved fatal. Jeannette went to see her in the hospital as soon as she heard of the accident, and asked her, "How long have you worn men's clothes, Dr. Walker?" "I never wore men's clothes," Dr. Walker replied. "I always wore my own."

** Harriet Sedman also managed the household on California Street, saving Jeannette stress and strain both at home and in her office. As their youngest sister, Edna McKinnon, tells, Harriet "closely resembled Jeannette, and could often entertain visitors who were curious simply to 'see' the first woman member of Congress."

Extra helpers were also needed when pamphlets from the various agencies or packets of seeds from the Department of Agriculture had to be distributed.

This unusually large staff was made necessary by the huge volume of mail that arrived at Jeannette's office, exceeding that of any congressman at the time; it came not only from Montana but from all over the country and from all parts of the world. "Often as much as two big canvas mail sacks full of letters were brought in in the morning," Belle Fligelman reported, "and each letter got an answer." Visitors streamed in from everywhere, some merely to be able to say that they had shaken hands with the new congresswoman, others to ask favors or press her with regard to some legislation. Mrs. Booth Tarkington arrived one day with a large handsome diary in which the staff was urged to make entries that would be of historical value later on. Unfortunately there never seemed to be enough time to do this. Then too there was the usual assortment of cranks or unfortunates who believed that there was nothing Jeannette could not accomplish: a man telephoned from a hospital one day to tell her that his leg was about to be amputated; if Jeannette would have him transferred to another hospital he was certain the leg could be saved.

Jeannette lost little time finding her way around from her office to the House chamber and in and out of committee rooms, and settled down to work. There was a great deal of legislation on the carpet in connection with the prosecution of the war, but she saw no point in making herself conspicuous by opposing all such measures once the die was cast. Like British Fabians such as George Bernard Shaw and Leonard Woolf, she believed that her country should not have gone to war, but once we were in it, she wanted our side to win; in the meantime she looked for ways to safeguard civil liberties and to prevent the erosion of recent social gains for women workers and children—common victims of martial fervor. She shared Jane Addams's conviction that "war itself destroys democracy wherever it thrives . . . not only in Russia and Germany but in the more democratic countries as well." Like Senator LaFollette, therefore, she voted against the Espionage Act, which as he had foreseen proved to be less an effective instrument against enemy infiltration than a limitation on freedom of thought. Her article in the *Ladies' Home Journal* of August 1917 on the subject of what women should do in wartime showed how apprehensive she was that factory reforms might be nullified. Remarking upon the fatuity of those who proposed, for example, that women should hand-grind their own flour in an economy drive, she pleaded for greater realism and broader social goals. "Carried along on the waves of a misguided patriotism," the article read, "have come subtle attempts to destroy the industrial standards of this country. . . ." These standards must be maintained, it went on to say, "and to ease the problems of vast numbers of working women engaged in war industries, we must keep up the schools, not curtail them, as some proposed; establish maternity care clinics and child welfare centers; provide public food kitchens."*

Aware that she had failed to make her position on the war issue clear to the people in April, she seized the chance to speak out in December, when Wilson called for a joint session of Congress to ask for a declaration of war against Austria-Hungary. By this time she felt so much at home in the House that she invited her two little nieces to sit beside her. One of them remembers that as the senators filed down the aisle in pairs to take their places Jeannette pointed out one proud figure who walked alone—Senator LaFollette. Jeannette's speech in the debate was short but precise:

> Mr. Chairman, I still believe that war is a stupid and futile way of attempting to settle international disputes. I believe that war can be avoided and will be avoided when the people, the men and women in America, as well as in Germany, have the controlling voice in their government. Today special commercial

* This article was ghosted for Jeannette by her friend Katharine Anthony, but its content shows close collaboration between the two old friends. Katharine spent several weeks at the California Street apartment while preparing the *Ladies' Home Journal* article. Although Jeannette all her life was a verbalizer, prolific in ideas, she had great resistance to writing, either out of diffidence or for lack of time to organize her ideas on paper. Everything that has appeared under her name in print represents her own thoughts, but the composition is that of others. This is in striking contrast to her speeches which, although extemporaneous, were well organized, well expressed, and very much to the point.

> interests are controlling the world. When we declared war on Germany we virtually declared war on Germany's allies. The vote we are to cast is not a vote on a declaration of war. This is a vote on a mere technicality in the prosecution of a war already declared. I shall vote for this, as I voted for money and men.

But even in routine war bills she was on the alert to help advance the cause of women's rights. An opportunity to secure equal employment practices for qualified women—a major plank in the women's liberation movement today—came in connection with the debate on the Lever Bill, a measure authorizing the secretary of agriculture to gather information on the production and conservation of food in wartime. On May 28, 1917, Jeannette delivered her first speech in Congress to offer an amendment to the Lever Bill, calling for the employment of women, so far as practicable, in the work provided for therein.

> Our higher educational institutions [she said] have been turning out a large body of women who are trained to deal with fundamentals from a scientific standpoint. It would be to the advantage of the government to utilize the services of trained women in the place where they would count the most for the country during this present crisis and in the future. . . . Women must take an intelligent and responsible share in the world's work if we are to see that all the people are fed all the time.

Her amendment passed. (The Lever Act, in its final form, was an important piece of legislation: it set up the Food Administration and as later amended provided for the fixing of food prices to resist inflationary and black-market pressures.) She was less successful in an attempt to alleviate the plight of impoverished women and children whose breadwinners were serving in the armed forces. On July 10 she introduced a bill appropriating $5,000,000 for separation allowances to dependent families of soldiers and sailors, but the measure was referred to the Committee on Military Affairs and never came to a vote.

Aside from acting as a lawmaker, there was another field where a representative in Congress could function in behalf of her constituents: in the scrutiny of various executive departments and agencies to make sure they were being conducted in accordance with the law. Soon after Jeannette gave her maiden speech, an opportunity presented itself to take bold action in defense of women in the civil service. Late in June a Montana woman whose sister was employed in the Bureau of Printing and Engraving, a branch of the Treasury Department, came to Jeannette with a tale of inhumane working conditions in the bureau, which was then operating full tilt turning out Liberty Bonds and paper money to pay for the war. Jeannette visited the bureau incognito, posing as the constituent of another congressman, to see the situation for herself. She found hundreds of young women working at high pressure as much as fifteen hours a day, or twelve hours on the night shift—although the eight-hour day had been established by law—some lifting and carrying huge stacks of paper, others examining every bill as it came off the presses for flaws in the engraving or mistakes in the numbers. For this exacting labor their pay was $625 a year, and contrary to civil service regulations no sick-leave or vacations were allowed, nor were the women permitted to ask for transfers to other positions for which they were qualified.

Deeming her own observations insufficient as evidence, Jeannette hired a professional investigator, Miss Elizabeth Watson, who had worked for the Factory Commission of New York State and the National Child Labor Committee, to help her make a case. Since Jeannette was not empowered to pursue her inquiry as a member of a regularly constituted congressional committee, her apartment in California Street became the headquarters of the investigation. Here one Sunday the women from the bureau came to state their grievances, while Miss Watson took their affidavits and made up a card index with information on all aspects of their work and pay, supplementing this with sworn statements from physicians and others about the effect of such conditions on the health of the women. Katharine Anthony came down from New York to help coordinate the material gathered.

Armed with this information, Jeannette called on Joseph Ralph, director of the bureau, and appealed to him to restore the eight-hour schedule as required by law. Ralph replied that it was impossible; he was short of help, and moreover, ninety percent of the women really preferred the long hours because they made extra money for overtime. (As Jeannette well knew, in every effort by labor to reduce working hours, employers stoutly maintained that the longer day was popular with the hired hands for this reason.) She reminded him that there were 500 names on the civil service list from which he could draw more help as he needed it. Ralph promised to do what he could to improve conditions, but after a few days it became apparent that he meant to make only token changes.

Jeannette thereupon went directly to Ralph's superior, Secretary of the Treasury McAdoo, with a bill of particulars, calling for an inquiry into the complaints of the bureau workers without delay and stating that she would release the affidavits to a congressional committee if he did not act promptly. McAdoo bowed to the threat and ordered a hearing for the next day. It needed only three hours of testimony for him to decide that the complaints were justified and to order the immediate restitution of the eight-hour schedule, vacations, sick leave, and the right to transfer to other positions in the government. Not long afterward Ralph resigned to become president of a banknote company, where no nosy congressman could pry into his operating methods, but before he left his post, Jeannette charged later, he did his best to demoralize the agency in order to prove that the eight-hour shift was unworkable.

The story of Jeannette's gumshoeing activities and her success in obtaining reforms in the Bureau of Printing and Engraving won favorable coverage in the press. A headline in the *New York Times* for July 2, 1917, read: "Miss Rankin Visits Bureau as Sleuth," and a later story gave a more detailed account of the whole affair. The insight Jeannette had gained into women's poor bargaining position in the government bureaucracy had another result: she encouraged Grace McNally to organize the women in the bureau, a drive that brought about the formation of the largest union of Federal employees in the United States up to that time. A year later Jeannette succeeded in having a bill providing for pay increases to men printers amended to include a minimum wage for their assistants, who as a rule were women.

Although Jeannette saw herself as the sole representative of women in Congress, she did not feel that she represented them only; other victims of the industrial system, regardless of sex, came within her province. Even during her clash with Ralph, matters of special concern to her working-class constituents in Montana had aroused attention across the country. On June 8 one of those tragic industrial accidents that provoke momentary shock and compassion in the great public took place in Butte, where more than 160 men were killed in a fire at the Speculator copper mine. There was no miners' union in Montana at the time, because the Company had effectively crushed their organization in 1914, but in the aftermath of the fire all the mine workers spontaneously went out on strike. Among other things they demanded a raise in pay and a change in the hiring system, by which the copper companies exercised a peculiarly autocratic control over the labor market. More moving still, and at the heart of the unrest, because it is a cry heard to this day after every mine disaster, was the demand that the state mine inspector be dismissed as a company stooge and that the laws for safety in the mines be observed.

Seizing the moment, the International Workers of the World (IWW), which for years had been trying to organize the unorganized in the West along syndicalist lines, in opposition to the craft unionism of the American Federation of Labor, now sent organizers into Montana to build a militant miners' union. Although its ideology was anarcho-syndicalist, the immediate aims of the IWW were simply to obtain better working conditions for the miners, and particularly a strict application of the safety rules already on the statute books. These fairly modest proposals were treated by the defenders of law and order as if the very foundations of society were threatened; Butte was placed under martial law, and Federal troops were summoned to preserve property, if not life. A mass meeting of the strikers unanimously approved a petition asking the Federal government to take over the mines "so that the miners may give prompt and practical evidence of their patriotism" in time of war.

The leader of the IWW in Butte was Frank Little, a veteran Wobbly, and no stranger to Montana, having been jailed in Missoula in 1909 for trying to unionize migrant laborers. Little was known as a tireless and effective organizer, but the hazardous life of a Wobbly had begun to take its toll; he was a sick man when he came to Butte in 1917. On August 1 gunmen broke into the hotel room where he was bedridden with a broken leg, tied him with ropes to the back of an automobile, dragged him through the streets, fired several bullets into his body and then hanged him from a railroad trestle. The vigilantes were nothing if not thorough.*

Having kept in close touch with events in her home state, especially since the disaster of June 8, Jeannette saw the justice of the miners' petition for a Federal takeover of the mines. The unchecked power of the Anaconda Copper Company in Montana and its stranglehold on the economy, the press, and the local government, were well known to her from her campaigns for suffrage and for election to Congress. In wartime few industries were more critical than the production of copper for bullets and shells, and if the Company would not provide safe, tolerable working conditions for the miners, the whole war effort might suffer a setback. Moreover, the government was already operating the railroads by now and had established wage and price controls in most industries.

To whom could she communicate the substance of the miners' petition? After making some inquires, she learned that Bernard Baruch, chairman of the War Industries Board, was the man to see, and she arranged to call on him. Baruch listened to her and then shook his head: there was nothing he could do; only the President could act in such a situation. Jeannette asked for an appointment to see the President. Wilson, courteous as usual, said he could give her no help: "All that is in the hands of Bernard Baruch. You must take it up with him."

"But I've just come from Bernard Baruch," she cried. "He told me I must take it up with you!"

Wilson laughed and threw up his hands. End of interview. Probably neither Wilson nor Jeannette knew that Baruch had had profitable business relations with the copper barons before taking his government post.

Frustrated in her attempt to get action from the administration,

* A major reason why Frank Little was hated out West, other than his being a Wobbly organizer, was that he was half Indian.

Jeannette decided to take the issue to Congress; on August 7 she introduced a resolution authorizing the President to requisition the copper mines for operation by the government and asked for time to present her case adequately. The President, she said, had been granted the power to commandeer practically every industry engaged in supplying war materials, except for nonferrous mines. Copper production had fallen off alarmingly owing to "disagreement" between mine operators and mine workers, and this had led to great lawlessness. "In Bisbee [Arizona]," she pointed out, "hundreds of men were deported in complete contempt of law and order. In Butte a man was lynched by masked men."

At the mention of the Butte lynching, Representative Johnson of Washington State leaped to his feet to ask if she would yield. "Did this man who was hanged," he asked, "belong to an organization which declares that it owes allegiance to no government?"

Miss Rankin. I understand that he belonged to the organization known as the Industrial Workers of the World . . .

Mr. Johnson. Is the lady familiar with the preamble and basic law of that outfit?

Miss Rankin. Yes; but this is a question of lawlessness. It is not a question of whom they hanged.

> I have tried [she continued] by every means that I know of to get governmental machinery in action to handle this deplorable situation in my state. I have kept in close touch with the situation in Butte. After the deportation occurred in Bisbee I received telegrams from Butte asking for Federal protection. I reported this to the Department of Labor and was informed that the department was doing all in its power to handle the situation through its representative, Mr. Rogers. A week ago last night I received a telegram at midnight saying that Mr. Rogers had left Butte, that no satisfactory settlement had been made, and that the people feared violence, and urged me to ask Secretary [of Labor] Wilson for protection. I telephoned this message to the Secretary at once. He asked me to see him the next day. I tried all the next day, until late in the evening, and was still trying to see the Secretary on Wednesday morning, when I received word that a man had been lynched.

> Then came more appeals for protection. I tried to see the President, the Department of Labor, the Department of Justice, and, finally, the War Department. . . . In a crisis of this kind . . . there should be some effective means by which the government would be able to protect itself against a decrease in productiveness, and by which the people of each state would be guaranteed the protection provided by the Constitution of the United States.

She went on to describe the grievances of the miners, telling how the Company had crushed the union, and gave details of the Company's hiring methods, called the "rustling-card system." This amounted to a blacklist in reverse, she said, for whenever a man applied for work in the mines his record was looked into to find out whether he had ever complained of his working conditions, or belonged to a labor union, or voted the wrong political ticket. If he was "clean," he was given a rustling card, and if he could not show such a card when applying for work, he was turned away. This system, she continued,

> has effectively discouraged the men from organizing. It has prevented them from demanding the enforcement of laws requiring safety devices in the mines. It has caused them to hesitate to discuss their grievances on the outside. The conditions of the mines have grown more and more unsafe. I have had heartbreaking letters from the wives of miners saying that when their husbands went to work they never knew whether or not they would return.

Toward the end of her speech Jeannette told of having made several futile appeals to John D. Ryan, president of the Anaconda Copper Company, to do away with the rustling-card system. Members might have noticed, she said, that Mr. Ryan had recently accepted an important post with the American Red Cross, but he had made no reply to her letters and telegrams asking for more humanitarianism in the copper mines.

Her speech was a remarkable performance, one that would have done credit to a congressman of long experience. But it did not sway the House, although at times she was interrupted by applause. As the situation continued to deteriorate in Montana, she decided that she might be able to bring peace to the area if she tried personal mediation in the strike. Arriving in Butte on August 14, she found both sides in the controversy on hand prepared to give her a proper reception, according to their lights. As her train rolled into the station, a huge crowd of sympathizers, estimated at 10,000, stood waiting to greet her, but owing to some peculiar arrangements, she was not permitted to show herself. Before she could leave her car a group of men whom she assumed to be members of a welcoming committee approached her and said: "This way, please." They led her down the train to the far end of the platform and into a waiting automobile, in which she was driven directly to her hotel. It was only then that she realized just what had happened. "I think you might say that I was kidnapped," she said later, adding that the men in the "welcoming party" obviously were Company agents who feared the effect of a demonstration in full view of the citizenry and the reporters.

Her "kidnappers" did her no harm, nor could they prevent her appearance the following evening at a public park, where she received a tremendous ovation. "I have no patience with the alleged utterances of Frank Little," she told an audience of thousands, "but I have the greatest contempt for the form of direct action that permitted the foul and cowardly murder of Frank Little!" And when she went on to say, "I am convinced that the demands of labor in this trouble are just and should be granted," the crowd stood and cheered her for fifteen minutes. Her brother said afterward that it was the most enthusiastic popular tribute anyone had received in Butte, "and it wasn't the miners alone. It was all the people."

"All the people" of Butte, nevertheless, proved to be impotent in a struggle with the mine owners. In the end the miners broke ranks as winter came on and began drifting back to work, unorganized, underpaid, with no safety guarantees. The Company made no concessions, nor did it forget its enemies. Jeannette did not slay the giant, but she had stood up to him.

In her August 7 speech in Congress on the Montana crisis, Jeannette expressed her regret that she was unable to address her colleagues on the question of woman suffrage at that time. Back again in Washington in the fall of 1917, she directed her efforts toward winning passage of a Federal amendment to give women the vote. On September 24 she asked for the floor to speak in favor of the Raker resolution, which provided for the establishment of a Committee on Woman Suffrage. Up to this time the suffrage amendment had been referred to the Judiciary Committee year after year, only to be bottled up there without ever coming to debate. To make sure that it received proper consideration, Congressman John D. Raker of California now asked that a special committee be set up, with the power to hold hearings at which proponents and opponents of the amendment could testify.

The debate on whether to set up this special committee gave Representative Meeker of Missouri a chance to air his antisuffragist views in a querulous speech studded with feeble shafts of sarcasm. Suffrage, he maintained, was a matter to be decided locally, by the states, and if it was to be considered in the House it should rightfully be referred to the Judiciary Committee. (He was a member of the Judiciary Committee.) He had had about as much of the feminist movement as he could stand, he expostulated; suffragists made nuisances of themselves, walking up and down the streets with a tin horn, and he was tired of their nagging persistence.

Thanks to Mr. Campbell of Kansas, who yielded his turn to speak next, Jeannette stood up to answer this somewhat less than statesmanlike utterance. She spoke calmly and judiciously. "Mr. Speaker," she said,

> I believe we should have a woman-suffrage committee in the House, as we have one in the Senate. . . . This is a question that should take all of the time of one committee. The Judiciary Committee has all it can do in attending to the regular business that comes before [it] . . . and we would like to have a committee that would discuss the merits of the question and would report either favorably or unfavorably. . . .

Then in answer to Meeker's argument that suffrage should be decided locally, she said:

> Some have told us to go to the states. Of course we have always known that woman suffrage was constitutional according to the Federal Constitution, but some of the state constitutions dis-

> franchise women. Perhaps it is news to you that some of the women in the United States can never be enfranchised except by a Federal amendment, for the constitutions of the states are such that it is practically impossible to amend them.

And she cited the case of New Mexico, where the obstacles to amending the constitution were almost insuperable, as well as Alabama, New York, Pennsylvania and New Jersey, where the procedure was complex and long-drawn-out.

The Raker resolution passed the House with a large majority, and Jeannette was named a member of the Committee on Woman Suffrage. She resisted a move to make her chairman of the committee in place of Raker, because she thought he would do a good job. He was a Democrat, to be sure, but if she, a Republican, were to replace him, some Democrats might be alienated, and every available Democratic vote was needed to win favorable consideration of the amendment.

But which amendment would the committee recommend? There was the Susan B. Anthony amendment: "The rights of citizens of the United States to vote shall not be denied or abridged by the United States or by any state on account of sex," which had the support of the National American Woman Suffrage Association and the majority of suffragist sympathizers, including Jeannette. There was also the Lucretia Mott amendment: "Men and women shall have equal rights throughout the United States and in every place subject to its jurisdiction," which was supported by Alice Paul and the National Woman's Party. The Woman's Party, though its membership—about 50,000—was small in comparison with that of the National Association, with nearly 2,000,000, had succeeded in raising large funds and had established headquarters opposite the White House. From this vantage point Miss Paul carried on her campaign for women's rights aggressively, giving the enemy no quarter. Sharing the point of view of leading British suffragists that the party in power should be held responsible, the Woman's Party opposed the election of men who favored suffrage if their party did not support it. Miss Paul believed that the President of the United States needed to be "educated" on the suffrage question; she sent delegations of women to him regularly to get him to take a positive stand. And with the flair of a press agent, she devised dramatic confrontations that made headlines all over the country. In December 1916, for example, on learning that President Wilson's address to Congress would contain no reference to the cause, she had a group of women enter the visitors' gallery of the House with parts of a banner (hidden under their long skirts) which they pinned together and flung over the railing just as Wilson was about to speak; it read: "Mr. President, what will you do for Woman Suffrage?"

A few weeks after passage of the Raker resolution, while the committee was considering how to frame their measure and what hearings should be held, Miss Paul set up a picket line of suffragists in front of the White House, a small group of women bearing banners and placards, a group constantly renewed, who stuck it out all day in sunshine or in driving rain. For several weeks the demonstration went on without hindrance, winning much attention in the press, until November 14, when the Washington police descended on the demonstrators and hustled them off to jail. The arrested women insisted that they be treated as "political prisoners"; in answer to this they were submitted to treatment not ordinarily borne by hardened criminals. Their first night in jail was described as "a night of terror."

When Lucy Burns, Miss Paul's associate, repeated that her constitutional rights were being violated, her jailers responded by chaining her lifted arms to the cell bars for hours. In the course of that "dreadful night," as the women described it, Dorothy Day, now known as the leader of the Catholic Workers group, was dragged into the station house, there to be hurled onto a bench and then thrown to the floor by the guards, who pummeled and kicked her without mercy. Others were thrown into rat-infested cells along with prostitutes and derelicts. As new recruits appeared on the picket line, they too were clapped into jail and sentences of from thirty to sixty days imposed. The women went on a hunger strike; their jailers resorted to forcible feeding. Alice Paul was given special treatment: the authorities claimed that she was insane, and although an alienist on the prison hospital staff declared her to be in her right mind, she was sent to the psychiatric ward, where a light was flashed in her face every hour of the night.

Jeannette felt great sympathy for the imprisoned women, although she herself believed in another line of action. When the scandalous conditions of their confinement became known, she made ready to visit them at the jail to see what she could do to help her sisters. The militants had been transferred from the District jail to the Occaquan Workhouse, however, and neither she nor Belle Fligelman knew how to get there. Recalling that a society woman of her acquaintance had spent a short time there as one of the White House pickets, she telephoned her for directions. "No, I don't know how to get there," said the woman. "I've only gone there in a Black Maria." Jeannette at length made her way to Occaquan, where she found the situation as bad as had been charged, although one circumstance had an element of black humor. The militant suffragists shared cells with prostitutes brought in from the street, but the prostitutes were dressed to the nines, while the women's rights prisoners insisted on wearing the gray prison garments, drab and shapeless, their hair uncombed and streaming down their backs. On her return to Congress Jeannette called for an investigation, but this was forestalled when all the demonstrators were released on December 3.

A month later, on January 3, 1918, the House Committee on Woman Suffrage opened hearings on the question of submitting a suffrage amendment to the Federal Constitution for ratification by the states, the Susan B. Anthony amendment recommended by the National Association. Witnesses in favor of the amendment were Dr. Anna Howard Shaw, Carrie Chapman Catt, and Maude Wood Park, who presented the usual arguments for equal franchise soberly and rationally. The entertainment, somewhat amateurish in character, was provided by the opposition, led by Mrs. James Wadsworth, national head of the antisuffragist party. Mrs. Wadsworth, the wife of a popular congressman from New York, was said to have some charm, even wit, but the witnesses she had brought with her were no tribute to her intelligence.

The first was a Dr. Lucien Howe, who testified that women should give their attention to their children, not to politics. To prove his point he quoted figures on the number of children suffering from "purulent diseases of the eye," diseases that resulted in blindness (he could not bring himself to utter the word "gonorrhea") because women didn't know enough to put a drop of silver nitrate in their babies' eyes at birth! "How do you expect women to know this disease when you do not feel it proper to call it by its correct name?" asked Jeannette, adding that in some states there were laws to prevent women from knowing anything about venereal diseases. "Do you think anything would shock women as much as blind children? Do you not think they ought to be hardened enough to stand the name of a disease when they can stand the fact that the children are blind?"

The next witness, Mrs. Wadsworth, tried to overcome the poor performance of Dr. Howe by taking a strong patriotic stand. An amendment providing for woman suffrage had been won in New York State the preceding fall, and it was Mrs. Wadsworth's claim that this had been achieved only with the support of Socialist, pacifist, and pro-German voters. To verify these allegations she introduced a Mr. Eichelberger, who showed charts and figures about the New York election. Jeannette challenged Mr. Eichelberger's statistical competence. "Are you the gentleman who compiled some figures on the Democratic and Republican women's vote in Montana last year?" she asked. "I think so." Jeannette: "Where did you get your figures?" Eichelberger: "From the official election report." Jeannette: "How could you tell a Democratic woman's vote from a Republican woman's vote?" Eichelberger: "Well, that part of it was just estimation."

With such lame witnesses for the antisuffragists, the committee lost little time in coming to a decision. On January 9 President Wilson announced that he was now in favor of a Federal amendment to give women the vote, and the next day a resolution calling for the submission of the suffrage amendment to the states for ratification was reported out to the House.

In deference to Jeannette's role in the movement, Chairman Raker asked her to open the debate. This was her great moment, the moment she had been waiting for ever since she had taken her seat in Congress, perhaps for longer than that, ever since she had addressed the Montana legislature in 1911. But she indulged in no histrionics, choosing rather to underscore the wider activities of women in wartime and the rising expectations of people the world over for the kind of democratic society the President had promised as a result of the war. "How shall we answer the challenge, gentlemen," she asked, "how shall we explain to them the meaning of democracy if the same Congress that voted to make the world safe for democracy refuses to give this small measure of democracy to the women of our country?"

Preliminary studies had indicated that though the tide was beginning to turn in favor of suffrage, the vote for the resolution would be very close, and on the basis of long experience Jeannette exerted herself to convince the undecided among her fellow congressmen, rather than spend time on the die-hard opponents of the resolution. There was one member, however, whom she thought it best to neutralize: Joe Walsh of Massachusetts, who had been loud in his antagonism to suffrage and to the seating of a woman in Congress as well. She had observed the man in action and could not close her eyes to the fact that he was a very able legislator, the sharpest among the Republicans to catch any violation of the rules and to block any irregularity by which the Democrats tried to slip some objectionable item into bills under consideration.

One weekend before the resolution was to come to a vote, she had an engagement to speak on suffrage in a city in Walsh's own district in Massachusetts. In the course of her talk there, she told his constituents that they were to be congratulated on the man they had chosen to represent them in Congress. She described how skillful he was in protecting their interests and in preventing Democratic skulduggery. "There is only one thing wrong with him," she said; "he is opposed to woman suffrage, and that is your fault. You have to convert him."

A couple of days later Walsh began receiving letters from his district advising him of Jeannette's amiable remarks. This made him quite uncomfortable, but courtesy demanded some acknowledgment, and with poor grace he called on her to thank her. As she recalls, however, he was so embarrassed he didn't know what to say. But the mere fact that he had made an approach of some kind nerved her to ask for a favor in return. When the suffrage resolution was about to come up for debate she went to him and said: "I don't expect you to change your mind about suffrage, but I want to ask you *not* to make a speech against it. You make such good speeches that you'll convince some of those who are undecided." Walsh could not bring himself immediately to agree to her request; he could only say that she was "giving him a hard time." After thinking it over, however, he decided not to take part in the debate.

The poor man was in fact putty in her hands. He performed still one more service for her, one of considerable subtlety. On the first roll call the resolution passed by only one vote, a margin too narrow for complacency. When the roll was called for the second time, Walsh went down to sit beside the clerk of the House, and to those he thought were going to change their vote from *for* to *against*, he said: "If you'll change your vote, I'll change mine." Jeannette was certain that this directness on his part kept all the members in favor of the resolution in line, for the vote was the same the second time around.

"He was my best friend from then on," Jeannette used to say. The resolution passed the House and then went to the Senate. There it failed to pass in that session, but the ground had been so well prepared that one year later a similar resolution was won in both houses, and by 1920 two-thirds of the states had approved an amendment to the Constitution lifting the sex restriction on the right to vote. Jeannette's part in this outcome was far from negligible, as much for the competence and astuteness she had shown as a congressman as for her earlier labors in the cause of woman suffrage.

Meanwhile there were other disabilities suffered by women to which Jeannette addressed herself. One day rather early in the session she had received a visit from Crystal Eastman,* a valiant suffragist and active social worker, who asked her to introduce a bill enabling women to retain their nationality after marriage to a citizen of another country. The handsome Miss Eastman was about to marry an Englishman and saw no reason why marriage should deprive her of the right to be an American. Jeannette was of the same mind, and in a speech she delivered before the National American Woman Suffrage Association's convention in the fall of 1917 she reported that she had already had such a bill put on the calender of the House.

* Crystal was the sister of Max Eastman, then editor of the socialist weekly *The Masses*.

> We who stand tonight so near victory after a majestic struggle of seventy long years [she said] must not forget that there are other steps besides suffrage necessary to complete the political enfranchisement of American women. We must not forget that the self-respect of the American woman will not be redeemed until she is regarded as a distinct social entity, unhampered by the political status of her husband or father, but with a status peculiarly her own and accruing to her as an American citizen.

This bill, known as the Rankin-Sheppard Bill, failed of passage during her term but was passed under other sponsorship in the next Congress.

An even more controversial piece of legislation introduced by her, known as the Rankin-Robertson Bill, suffered a similar fate. It was a bill for whose passage Julia Lathrop, head of the Children's Bureau, had been agitating for many years, and which Jeannette had promised Miss Lathrop she would introduce when they had met at the Shoreham Hotel breakfast on April 4. It provided for instruction in female hygiene, venereal disease, maternity and child care, as well as "education in the processes of life," a euphemism for birth control. Jeannette herself admitted that it had extremely limited application, but still it did not win congressional approval in the Sixty-fifth Congress. It did pass, however, in the Sixty-sixth, as the Sheppard-Towner Act. Although the section on education in birth control was far from a plan to encourage libertinage, it won Jeannette a new group of adversaries, among them many women who maligned her more fiercely than did many men. The sensibilities of some of the bill's opponents were offended by the mere naming of venereal diseases by a spinster; surely this betrayed impurity of mind! Jeannette would counter such charges by saying that the government had always provided instruction in the hygiene of pigs; why not human beings?

Jeannette went her own way undismayed, responding energetically to every challenge, tilting not at windmills but at fortresses of reaction and privilege. Some of the strongholds she attacked were to crumble within her lifetime; others remained impregnable, a constant spur to her fighting spirit. She had said that she considered *all* the women and children in the United

States as part of her constituency, and within the district she represented, the copper miners could also expect her to speak for them in Congress. But her concerns went far beyond the boundaries of state or nation. In January 1918 she introduced a resolution in the House calling for the United States to recognize "the right of Ireland to political independence and that we count Ireland among those countries for whose freedom and democracy we are fighting." By no flight of the imagination could the Irish rebels be included in her constituency, save for the fact that the Irish were an oppressed people. Nor was there a large bloc of Irish-Americans in Montana whose votes she courted by her stand. This challenge to the sincerity of our war aims evoked a moderate amount of editorial comment in the press, but little else.

It had an unexpected and significant effect, however, on Jeannette herself. Not long after her introduction of the resolution on Ireland, some East Indians called on her to ask why she did not express an equal interest in the cause of Indian independence. For all the wide range of her concerns, she realized that she knew little about the subcontinent that was the jewel in the crown of the British Empire. It was by then too late for her to do anything about it in Congress, but her interest was aroused to such a degree that she began to read all she could about the Indian problem, a course of study that was to lead her, by way of Gandhi, to the formulation of her own pacifist philosophy.

Jeannette Rankin's first term in Congress proved her to be easily the peer of most of her colleagues in the House. She had not succeeded in bringing about any earth-shaking changes, but she had set in motion several reforms, such as suffrage, that were soon to win acceptance; she had taken her stand on the great question of war and peace; she had pleaded the cause of ill-used workers in the copper mines and in the Federal bureaucracy; above all, she had shown by her actions that women were as well qualified as men to hold office and help make the laws of the land. Not until the advent of Shirley Chisholm and Bella Abzug was the House to know the presence of so purposeful a woman.

Because of her championship of humane causes, she was of course accused of naïveté, fanaticism, and lack of diplomacy. It is true that she did not master the art of political compromise by which legislators are accustomed to giving way on one high principle in order to achieve what they claim is a still-higher good. But she was not above resorting to guile to disarm an opponent, as in the case of Joe Walsh described earlier. (If you can't win over an opponent, immobilize him.) If she had common ground with any political group, it was more likely with the Populists; like them she believed in private property, but thought the system needed radical reforms to protect the people from the dominance of bankers and trusts. There was a narrowness in the Populist program, however, that was alien to her wider view of human affairs. Perhaps the charge that she was naïve had some basis in fact, but if a belief that "the people" need only learn "the truth" to act with reason and humanity is naïve, it is one shared by most politicians, at least in their public utterances.*

Paramount in her credo was an abiding faith in the democratic system as developed in the United States, despite the ambiguities of the two great political parties. She preferred to remain in the Republican fold, voting as a Republican in Congress on all issues where her principles permitted. When her term was about to expire, however, she found that the Republican party placed no great value on her voting record. Wellington had been right; she had jeopardized her career by voting against our entrance into the war. But it was not only this that convinced the Republican machine in Montana to get rid of her; it was more particularly her championship of the copper miners in a state where the Company dominated both parties.

Political hacks went about the state saying: "Do you want to *keep* a woman in Congress?" And to make it harder for her to win reelection, the Company-dominated legislature in its last

* It must be admitted that on one subject her judgment was not unwarped: Theodore Roosevelt. When he died she gave a short eulogy of the former President in the House, extolling him as a model for the youth of America. Perhaps she was influenced in this by Wellington's idolatry of T.R., but it is hard to understand her praise of a man who rated the military virtues above all else, who had volunteered to serve in one of America's least justified wars, and who as President had hugely expanded the navy, besides "taking Panama," as he himself boasted. Jeannette would have described him differently some years later.

session divided the state into two congressional districts, thus doing away with the congressman-at-large, and gerrymandering what would be Jeannette's district so that it contained an overwhelming number of Democratic voters. (Some years later the Supreme Court ruled that ten more counties should be added to her district to obtain more equitable representation of both parties.)

Jeannette nevertheless felt committed to seek reelection in 1918 on the basis of her performance in Congress, however dim her chances. Since it was unlikely that she could retain her seat in the House in a dominantly Democratic district, she decided to run for the Senate, which would allow her to canvass the whole state rather than a circumscribed district where the cards were stacked against her. She therefore entered her name in the Republican primaries, running along with three men who had the approval of the machine. Using Red-scare tactics, Company-controlled newspapers assailed her viciously, while party hirelings advised their followers to vote for any other candidate than Jeannette Rankin. In spite of all this, she came in second in the primaries, losing to Dr. Oscar M. Lanstrum, a perennial office-seeker whose "regularity" was unquestionable.

At this juncture she found herself in a painful dilemma. A third party, calling itself the National Party, which had just been founded by a group of Socialists, Progressives, and Farmer-Labor people who favored the war, had written in her name on the primary ballot, making it possible for her to run under their banner if she chose to do so. Under such auspices the chances of victory against the two entrenched parties were extremely slim, and the prospect of making an arduous campaign for nothing was not very appealing. But then an incident characteristic of Montana politics in those days made her decide to run.

The Democrats that year had renominated Senator Thomas J. Walsh, a widely respected liberal who was later to win fame when he uncovered the great Teapot Dome scandal. Earlier in his career Walsh had been a strong critic of the Anaconda Copper Company, along with Burton K. Wheeler, an associate in his law firm. It was common knowledge that Walsh could not have won his Senate seat in 1912 without the tacit acquiescence of the Company; Wheeler, however, continued to flaunt his independence of the copper barons. In 1918 the Company decided to tighten the screws on the senator and pressured him to make Wheeler call off his pro-labor campaign. When Walsh submitted, the Company threw its political and financial weight behind him in the Senate race.*

Walsh's action alienated so many liberals among his followers that it was feared Jeannette would draw votes away from him and lessen his chances of victory if she entered the contest. Democratic leaders in the state were terrified; they charged the Republicans with secretly encouraging her to run in order to win the senate seat for Lanstrum; they tried to bring pressure on Wellington to urge her to stay out; and in a last desperate move someone suggested to Walsh that a rumor be spread to the effect that she was bribed by the Republicans to withdraw. "Bribes are not offered in such a way that you can prove them," she told a friend later, "and in order to prove that I didn't accept a bribe I had to run. So I ran, knowing, of course, that there was no chance of being elected."**

She campaigned actively on a platform that embodied her often-expressed convictions, along with a few Populist planks probably supplied by her sponsors. "Win the war and make the world safe for humanity," was one of her slogans. And "Establish democracy at home, based on human rights as superior to property rights," was another. Her platform also called for national woman suffrage, Prohibition, Federal price support for farm products and an end to speculation in grain, as well as the elimination of all "unfair profiteering combinations."

But, as she had foreseen, it was a hopeless battle. The Populists were not strong in Montana except on the silver issue; the Socialists were negligible; while Walsh had the backing not only

* Wheeler himself was later to come to terms with the Company before he won his seat in the Senate in 1922.

** This story, somewhat obscure, is borne out by a letter in the files of Senator Walsh (cited by Ronald Schaffer) from a former lieutenant-governor named A. E. Spriggs, "a no-account man," according to Jeannette. She was especially indignant because Wellington was said to have been involved in the deal. Walsh himself paid no attention to Spriggs's suggestion, but the damage was done.

of the Company but also of other powerful interests, such as the three continental railroads and the large cattle owners. On Election Day in 1918 a violent storm blew up, keeping many voters at home. The influenza epidemic then raging throughout the country added to the number of absentees from the polls. Senator Walsh won easily, and although Jeannette's term in the House ran until March of the following year, she was a lame duck, for all practical purposes out of politics, and out of a job.

VII

Finding a New Base

The Lady from Montana left Congress in March 1919 with very real regret. In truth she had enjoyed every minute of her term, notwithstanding the strains she had endured because of her opposition to the war; she had relished the hard work, much of which had been undertaken at her own initiative; and she had taken unreserved pleasure in the power her office gave her to publicize issues that cried out for action. Fifty years later she said she felt that she had never left Congress: in spirit she was always there, attending its debates, worrying about its unfinished business, voting with Ernest Gruening and Wayne Morse against the Tonkin Gulf resolution. On the last day of the session she asked for the floor to make a little farewell speech in which she thanked her fellow representatives for their courtesy and expressed her sorrow that she was obliged to leave before the suffrage amendment passed both Houses. Privately she conceded that while the country was at war there had been little time for constructive legislation.

Two things saved her from a feeling of depression when she gave up her seat: first, her firm belief that her legislative career was not over, that she might still return to Congress one day as the member from Montana; and second, her sense that there was important work for her to do as a woman and a pacifist in other fields. Not in the suffrage movement, however, for the suffragists were in clear sight of victory, which was to come the following year when after a hard fight in Tennessee the requisite two-thirds of the states approved the Nineteenth Amendment to the Constitution. Armed with the vote, Jeannette thought at that time, women could put an end to war. Her favorite sociologist, Benjamin Kidd, in his book *The Science of Power*, had written that women instinctively and instantly tend to take the side of principle rather than interest, considering the race more important than the individual and the future greater than the present. She had earlier been struck by Kidd's phrase "the emotion of an ideal," which corresponded so closely to her own motivations, and she now believed fervently that she could help in bringing women to understand how they could function to prevent a repetition of the horrors of World War I, to make it in fact the last war. If Jeannette's view of women's instinctual responses seems rather exalted, it is well to remember that for a decade she had been closely associated with those of her sex who were leaders in all the current movements for social reform, "do-gooders," women of exemplary altruism and dedication, women who, like her, deplored injustice, cruelty and war and were willing to work without stint to correct such evils.

World War I had ended, and the great Allied politicos were sitting at Versailles to parcel out the spoils of victory while pretending to establish a permanent peace. Not many of those reading in their daily papers of these solemn deliberations were aware of the wheeling and dealing, the crass bargaining and the subtle blackmail carried on in the name of peace in the mirrored halls of the great palace. Even in the victorious nations, however, a few voices were raised to protest the betrayal of Wilson's Fourteen Points, to question the imposition of intolerable reparations on the former enemies, and to challenge the creation of a League of Nations that excluded certain countries and had no power to prevent future wars.

Among these critics were many of Jeannette's friends and associates. American women of pacifist leanings had already shown solidarity with like-minded women of Europe in their abortive attempt in 1915 to negotiate an end to the war; and some of them had embarked with Rosika Schwimmer on Henry Ford's ill-fated

Peace Ship. In the spring of 1919 they prepared to meet again with their counterparts overseas to try to snatch peace from the jaws of victory. Jeannette was named one of six American delegates to the Women's International Conference for Permanent Peace which was to be held in Zurich in May, a group including such eminent persons as Jane Addams of Hull House; Lillian Wald, founder of the Henry Street Settlement in New York; Florence Kelley, head of the Consumers League, who had drawn up the first factory inspection laws in the country; Lucia Ames Mead, lifelong peace propagandist; Emily Greene Balch, distinguished professor of economics (later Nobel Peace Prize winner); and Dr. Alice Hamilton, who had established the study of industrial diseases as a branch of medical science.

When the delegation embarked on the Holland-America liner *Noordam* on April 9, a ship's reporter for the *New York Times* interviewed Jeannette about her plans. In answer to his questions she said that she intended to "place the problem of stopping the spread of Bolshevism" before the Conference, adding that she expected "to receive many suggestions from the delegates who come from the countries where it is prevalent." She said too that she would press for support of laws safeguarding the original citizenship of women who married men of another country, and acknowledged that the subject of the League of Nations, "from a woman's standpoint," would also receive close attention at the Conference.

On board ship there were lively discussions among the delegates about the matters to be taken up in Zurich, discussions in which the issue of Bolshevism figured less prominently than Jeannette had supposed. The former congressman, who at the age of thirty-nine was the youngest member of the American delegation, and a novice in international affairs, had little to say in the company of her more experienced colleagues. At one point, however, Lucia Ames Mead raised the question of how women in the former enemy countries could be made to understand the larger issues with respect to war and its prevention, and Jeannette spoke up for the first time. "We don't want to tell them how to think," she declared. "We want to give them the facts so that they will know how to think." This remark, so characteristic of Jeannette's approach to political realities, struck Florence Kelley as most discerning and led to a closer association between the two soon afterward.

For most of this, her first trip to Europe, Jeannette traveled as the companion of Miss Addams, but when they reached Paris Miss Addams assigned her to share a room at the hotel with Mary Church Terrell, the celebrated black educator, an arrangement that caused some women in the party to raise their eyebrows. Even in this enlightened group there were women who did not instinctively take the side of principle, it would seem. Jeannette herself was color-blind about skin pigment. From Paris the American delegation made a five-day tour of the devastated regions, where the mutilated land made vivid the millions of men who had died there, and gave their mission a dreadful urgency.

Proceeding to Zurich, they were joined by women from all over Europe, women from Germany and Austria, from the victorious nations and from the neutrals, all asking themselves how they could prevent a repetition of the war that had just ended. It was not easy for those from the former enemy countries to attend this conference, where all in a sense were in the ranks of the defeated; attendance even by women from the victorious nations was viewed with indifference or outright opposition by their governments. Jeannette remembered one Italian delegate who had to pretend that she wanted to catch up on the latest fashions in millinery in order to obtain a passport.

On May 13 Miss Addams presided at the opening session of the Conference before some 100 delegates from thirteen countries. Jeannette was appointed chairman of the Feminist and Press committees. Quickly, soberly, without fanfare, the women went to work on an analysis of the terms of the peace treaty being contrived at Versailles and, with more prescience than was shown by the men assembled there, deplored the rapacity of the conquerors, in violation of stated principles (no indemnities, no reparations, Wilson had promised); the redrawing of national boundaries, in many cases so arbitrary as to ensure future international disputes; and the fragile structure of the League of Nations. Before adjourning they sent a delegation to Paris to present their findings to the negotiators at Versailles, along with an address to President Wilson proposing modification of the treaty. Wilson's courteous reply indicates only too clearly his feelings of discouragement and powerlessness:

> Your message appeals both to my intellect and to my heart, and I sincerely desire that means may be found to comply with it, although the prospects are far from reassuring because of the immense practical difficulties.

The women too knew that they were powerless to change the terms of the treaty, but they could at least speak their minds and hope for an echo in the minds of the millions who had paid so dearly for the war.

The last act of the Conference was to form itself into the Women's International League for Peace and Freedom, which has survived to this day through other wars, the longest-lived peace organization in the world, though no more effectual than any other. Jeannette was named vice-chairman of the Executive Board and served the League in one capacity or another for many years. Not much had been accomplished in Zurich, but a bond had been forged among peace-loving women of all nations, and for Jeannette at least the challenge of bringing states and peoples together to accept peaceful solutions of their differences was an enticement to action. Since she never believed that this could be accomplished through the League of Nations as it had been set up in Paris, she suffered no letdown when President Wilson failed to win its acceptance by the Senate.

Not many months after her return from Europe, however, she must have been taken aback when she learned to what degree her fears about "the spread of Bolshevism" expressed to reporters before she sailed were shared by officials of the United States government. The Palmer raids on radicals and dissidents of every description in 1920, their arrest without warrant and their imprisonment without trial showed a paranoia on the subject that she was immune to, and led to her joining the American Civil Liberties Union, of which she became vice-president. Neither did the election of Warren Harding as President and the installation of his poker-playing friends in positions of power encourage her to believe that the prospect for enlightened government was favorable.

But she was not downhearted. In 1920 she was forty, in good health and spirits, conscious that she had already played a part of some significance in the country's history, and ready to embrace some new project that would use her energies and have some larger meaning. Her trip to Europe, coming immediately after her term in Congress ended, had been a welcome distraction for her. Besides enlarging her horizons, it had permitted her to postpone for the moment a decision on what she would do next.

During the twenties, that period of hectic surface prosperity and hollow boom, she worked principally as a lobbyist for various causes that required her presence either in Washington or in the states east of the Mississippi. Montana therefore ceased to be practical as a base for her operations, although she continued to return there for the summer months and holidays. (By passing the summer at Wellington's ranch, she admitted openly, she was able to save money on her living expenses, an important consideration in view of her small income and intermittent employment.) In Montana, moreover, she was a member of the Rankin clan; her brother Wellington was one of the most prominent men in the state, and some of her sisters had already carved out independent careers. Harriet Sedman, the closest to Jeannette in age, after serving as Jeannette's secretary in Washington had returned to Missoula to become Dean of Women at Montana State University; Mary had taught English at the University for some years, then married Herbert Bragg, and was now the mother of a daughter and a son; Edna, the first woman born in Montana to win a law degree (although she never practiced), having married John W. McKinnon, Jr., had a young son and daughter; and Grace, now Mrs. Thomas E. Kinney, had a family of three children, two boys and a girl. They were all thus established on their own and were somewhat detached from their old home, but when Jeannette returned to Montana as the unmarried daughter she would be expected to live with her mother and adapt herself to a pattern of domestic life from which she had escaped when she went to Congress. Mrs. Rankin was a lively and intelligent old woman, but in her own house she was the "matriarch," as her daughter Edna described her; she insisted, for example, that all her grandchildren be born there, wherever

Rankin family group in 1920. Back row, left to right: Harriet (Sedman); Mary (Bragg); Wellington; Edna (McKinnon), holding her daughter Dorothy; Grace (Kinney); Jeannette. Second row: Mary Elizabeth and Virginia Sedman. Third row: Janet Kinney, next to her grandmother; Olive Rankin, holding Thomas Kinney. Fourth row: John Kinney; Kenneth Bragg. In foreground: Mary Jane Bragg.

their parents might be living. Affectionate though her relations were with all the members of her family, it was important for Jeannette to cut the cord, to confirm her independence by a way of life after her own pattern.

The affluent arrangements at Wellington's Avalanche Ranch did not correspond to Jeannette's life style, which had a rugged character more reminiscent of her childhood. There was in effect very little for her to do, and hers was the kind of mechanism that needed constant operation to keep it in good repair. Only one incident of life there stood out in her memory as requiring some affirmative action. Like all establishments where horses are daily companions, Wellington's had one spirited stallion that was a universal favorite because of his prankishness as well as his beauty. One day he broke out of the corral when there was no one at the house to go in pursuit but Jeannette. Saddling her own horse, a gentle mare, she took out after the runaway over the fields and hills and found him at last cropping the grass placidly many miles away. He submitted without demur to her tying a halter around his neck, but when she tried to mount her own horse to return home, he would not have it. Again and again she tried to get into the saddle, but each time he blocked her, interposing his head or his whole body between her and the stirrup. As the afternoon was wearing on, in the end she let him have his way and made the long trek home on foot, leading the two horses by rope and bridle, the stallion now amiably accompanying her with what must have been a grin on his handsome face.

In 1923 she bought a farm of sixty-four acres in Georgia and put up a house there. Why Georgia? One can only assume that a person who had traveled as widely as she had over the length and breadth of the country must have had particular reasons for settling in an area so different from the one in which she had been born and raised. The melting sweetness of the Georgia spring, which comes so early in the year with its daffodils and magnolias and peach blossoms? The courtesy and warmth of its people? One reason may have been its accessibility to Washington, where to Jeannette's mind much of the action was; moreover, Bogart, the village where she settled, was only ten miles from Athens, the seat of the state university, where she was sure to find agreeable companionship and possible sympathy for her views, and not above fifty miles from Atlanta, the state capital. If she was to build up a new constituency, a constituency committed to peace, this might be a good place to start.

Her own explanation of the move to Georgia was that she had found the South congenial ever since her early trips there as a suffrage worker. Southerners in the main were opposed or indifferent to woman suffrage, but on the other hand she sensed a stronger current of anti-war feeling than in other parts of the country in consequence of their greater suffering during the Civil War. This impression was confirmed by the attitudes of southern congressmen during the debate on the declaration of war in 1917, when Claude Kitchin, for example, had spoken so eloquently against the resolution. Some years later she said that she liked working in the South because southerners were "interested in humanity more than in cold dollars"; the South, she declared, had no big industry with a selfish interest in promoting wars.* No doubt it also occurred to Jeannette that the politics of Georgia might be more plastic than in her own state, where a single giant corporation exercised practically sovereign powers. Although some may think it odd, considering her enlightened attitude toward minorities of all races, that she was not dissuaded from settling in the South by the Negro problem, or that, once there, she did not ally herself with the civil rights movement, it must be remembered that she had been reared in close proximity to another oppressed group—the Indians—and while she was aware of the injustices of the situation, she was not prepared to offer solutions. Throughout her life she tended to give herself to one great cause at a time, and, while involved in that, to avoid weakening her impact by attacking on several fronts.

Jeannette's good friend Katharine Anthony spent a month in the summer of 1925 at the farm in Bogart and wrote a series of articles for the *Woman's Home Companion* describing the plain living and high thinking that characterized the place, fortunately not to the exclusion of good cheer. Miss Anthony did not name the former congresswoman whose home she was visiting but referred to her as Aspasia, after the brilliant consort of Pericles the Athenian. "Aspasia's farm," she wrote, "was once a famous dewberry patch. Aspasia is a pioneer. She would never buy a farm which others had cultivated. She likes to blaze trails for others to follow and plough new lands for others to cultivate." The dewberry, a form of blackberry, has little to recommend it

* In the twenties this was a reasonable assessment, but within the next two decades Georgia's industrial development brought it into the mainstream of American capitalist enterprise, where humane values seem to get lost.

aside from its fruit, which is fairly troublesome to pick, and although Jeannette allowed some of the bushes to remain, she had enough of the land cleared to plant a grove of young pines and 200 pecans, as well as a fig tree, a chinaberry tree, and a persimmon near the well; the rest of the acreage was covered with trailing honeysuckle, wild cherry, wild plum, grapevines and dogwood.

"The place was not exactly a wilderness," Katharine Anthony observed. "It was, I suppose, about as wild as the Garden of Eden must have been." The only building Jeannette found standing on the farm was a small shed or "cotton house," which she converted into a kitchen, attached to the main house by a gangway.

The dwelling Miss Anthony saw in 1925 consisted of one long room and a screened sleeping porch, the room heated by a contraption of Jeannette's devising as ingenious as a Rube Goldberg cartoon engine except that it actually functioned. From the open hearth at one end she installed water pipes to the other end, where they were attached to an old car radiator. In chilly weather the logs burning in the fireplace warmed the water in the pipes so that the heat was distributed throughout the room. Meals were brought in from the kitchen and served from a three-tiered cart; dishes were washed under a tree near the well, amid the fragrance of flowers and ripening fruit. In such close quarters every activity had to be carefully planned and allotted, for Jeannette was happiest when her house was filled with visiting friends and relatives. Visitors were in fact so numerous that she was obliged to add four bedrooms to the main building, as her niece, Dorothy Brown, recalls:

> two upstairs, two down, with a spiral staircase so narrow that my grandmother got her corsets stuck in the top opening the first and only time she went up to look, and we had a hell of a time getting her pried loose. . . . I . . . remember the outhouse in Bogart. I felt very sorry for myself, since we had *The Nation* and *The New Republic* for toilet paper, and very rough paper it was, while all our neighbors wiped on catalogues with slick paper.

This was pushing plain living and high thinking a little too far. By some incongruity the place was named "The Tepee," as if the owner might pull up stakes and move on to other hunting grounds at any moment, which was far from the case.

She was at first regarded with some curiosity or suspicion by her neighbors, but she soon made friends with the wives of all the farmers round about, "proselytizing" them, as Miss Anthony relates, in the interests of peace. She also started a club for girls, originally for the purpose of teaching them to swim, and a club for boys, ostensibly for their entertainment, but in reality to expose the young folks to new ideas. The Boys' Club survived for many years, until all the charter members had become grown men, burdened with family responsibilities, yet always loyal to Jeannette.

If Jeannette supposed that her pecan trees would provide her in time with a subsistence, she was soon disabused of the notion. Her poor white neighbors, working their small cotton fields and corn patches, raising a few chickens and pigs, could barely make ends meet and keep their children in shoes. Jeannette imitated their thrift by canning and preserving all the fruits, berries and vegetables that grew on the place, more out of a hatred of waste than a need for such strict economy. With her private income of $75 a month she was in no danger of want; the Spartan regime she had outlined for herself was designed rather to secure the freedom to do what she wanted to do, unfettered by useless acquisitions or the need for display.

The first job she tackled after her return from Zurich had stressed her need for a base of operations closer to the eastern seaboard than Montana. In 1920 Florence Kelley offered her the post of field secretary of the National Consumers League; she was to function as a lobbyist for the passage of social welfare legislation in Washington, particularly the Sheppard-Towner Bill. This was the very bill that Jeannette had introduced in the Sixty-fifth Congress, calling for Federal grants to the states for instruction in female hygiene in order to reduce the maternal and infant death rate. Since the membership in Congress had not been changed too radically by the elections of 1918 and 1920, she knew which men were committed in favor of or against the bill, and what arguments could be brought to bear on the undecided. She herself appeared to testify at the committee hearings, along with Julia Lathrop and Florence Kelley, two eloquent advocates. The measure was passed by both Houses in November 1921.

Florence Kelley next sent her to Chicago to represent the Consumers League in a multistate campaign to improve working conditions in factories through regulatory legislation of the kind in which New York State had pioneered ten years earlier. Jeannette organized the Mississippi Valley Conference for Labor and Welfare Legislation, with headquarters at Hull House. From there she went out into six states, addressing Rotary Clubs, chambers of commerce, trade unions and women's groups in support of bills for factory reform and workmen's compensation, but although she succeeded in having bills introduced in the various legislatures, they either died in committee or were voted down. The end of the war had brought about a high rate of unemployment, caused in part by the halt in war production and in part by the return of the veterans; this in turn had weakened the labor movement, which would otherwise have been more effective in supporting the program.

Her next assignment was also abortive. In May 1924 the Consumers League called her to Washington to lobby for passage of a constitutional amendment to prohibit child labor. Along with other welfare organizations at that time, the League held to the belief that as in the case of woman suffrage a constitutional amendment prohibiting child labor would accomplish at one stroke what would otherwise take long-drawn-out campaigns for many years in the state legislatures. Jeannette lobbied vigorously on both sides of the Capitol for the resolution to submit the amendment to the states, and had the satisfaction of seeing it pass in both Houses. The joy of the reformers was short-lived, however, for the amendment won approval in only a few states and was never again brought forward, although Florence Kelley pressed for it obstinately and fruitlessly almost to the end of her life. One of her schemes was to get up a petition with millions of signatures—as in the suffrage campaign—to secure passage of the amendment. This campaign failed, while it diverted much of the energy that might have been directed to more realizable goals, and contributed to the decline of the Consumers League as a reform agency. Although Jeannette had enjoyed her four years with the League, working with congenial associates on projects that interested her, possibly she was already looking for a way out when she received a call from her brother Wellington. Would she come back to Montana and help him in his campaign for the United States Senate? Of course she would. Out of the lobbies and on to the hustings, talking to the people—that was where she loved to be. Her resignation from the League was not official until October 1924, but she had effectively separated herself from it in June of that year.

Loyalty and affection bound all the members of the Rankin clan, but with none of her siblings was Jeannette more closely allied than with Wellington, who had provided such loving support for her own career. Wellington had started out in law practice in Helena in the office of Senator Walsh, and two years later he put up his own shingle, becoming one of the most successful criminal lawyers in Montana. His practice was also concerned with cattlemen, which made him independent of the copper company and gave him the liberty to support Jeannette in her repeated controversies with the mining interests.

Like Jeannette he loved the political arena with all its calculated maneuvers and stratagems, its hard-fought electoral contests. He was an able public speaker; some called him a spellbinder. As time went on he became a power in the Montana Republican party, serving as chairman of the Executive Committee, chairman of the Finance Committee, and national committeeman. Eventually he won election as the state's attorney general, and later as an associate justice of the Montana Supreme Court; later still he was appointed United States Attorney for the District of Montana. But what he yearned for most was a role on the national stage. His first attempt was to enter the primaries for a seat in Congress in 1922; it failed. Two years later, in 1924, he tried again, this time declaring his candidacy for the Senate, and won the nomination without difficulty. For the ardors of the campaign, however, he felt that he needed Jeannette, whose usefulness in swinging the women's vote, as well as the miners', might be crucial in his bid for election.

But even with Jeannette by his side it was a hopeless battle. His Democratic opponent was the incumbent, Senator Walsh, who was rounding out his second term in the Senate as a national figure of considerable stature, having just completed his exposure of the Teapot Dome frauds. Wellington was a man of charm, personable, honest, intelligent, but perhaps lacking the charisma needed for a successful political career. Walsh won reelection easily. Wellington was to try again for a high electoral office in 1928, when he aimed for the governorship, and once more in 1944, when he ran for the Senate a second time, but in neither case did he carry the day.

Jeannette returned to Georgia to settle into her new home and get better acquainted with her neighbors. Along with her resettlement had come a reordering of her own priorities, based on what she conceived of as her special mission. Without relinquishing her interest in social reforms, she was moving toward an attack on the central issue for modern society–the abolition of war as a means of settling international disputes–without which the most laudable reforms were a mockery and a delusion.

Her pacifist views were beginning to take on sharper definition; while clinging to her "emotion of the ideal," the ideal being peace, she was coming to believe that there was an important distinction between those who piously *longed for peace*, and those who were resolutely *opposed to war.* Peace-lovers could make excuses for an ongoing war, hoping that the next peace treaty would end war forever, but those who opposed war would go to any length to prevent that next war from breaking out. Fear of their neighbors made nations arm, and armaments gave them the pretext to settle their disputes by war. "When I first came to Georgia," she used to tell, "I would lock the door, and then at night I would hear every pine cone that fell. One night I forgot to lock the door and I didn't hear the pine cones [falling]. Locking the door was what frightened me."

Between 1925 and 1929 she associated herself with two peace groups in the hope that they might provide a workable program for preventing wars; neither was equal to the task as she saw it. The first was with the Women's International League for Peace and Freedom, with which she had been connected since its inception in Zurich in 1919. Early in 1925 she accepted a post as field secretary for the League, agreeing to go on a speaking and organizing tour similar to those she had made in the suffrage campaign. She spoke in Dayton, Ohio, saying, among other things: "No woman can with honor ask her son to go to war unless she can say that she has done everything in her power to prevent the necessity of making such a sacrifice." In Denver, Colorado, she took the position that war would be outlawed when there was universal woman suffrage throughout the world. In St. Louis she felt obliged to deny charges that the Women's International League for Peace and Freedom was linked with political radicalism; it was not true, she said, that the League was associated in any way with Socialism, Communism, Bolshevism, or the IWW.

It was not a successful trip; moreover, she was vexed by what she considered poor planning on the part of the League's staff. As early as February, before starting out on her tour, she wrote to Dorothy Detzer, Secretary of the League: "Will you please correct the minutes which says that my health will not permit my taking up organization work. My health is perfect. The conditions under which the work was proposed to be done would ruin the health of anyone who attempted it." And in a letter of April 18 she complained of the travel schedule drawn up by the staff, charging that her trip to St. Louis had been so poorly plotted that she had no prior information on train connections and found herself stranded in a town far from her next speaking engagement. "Am tired and discouraged over the waist [*sic*] of money and energy . . . If I had names and correspondance [*sic*] and material to work with I could have done more." The money provided by the League for her travel expenses also proved to be inadequate. But what was most frustrating to Jeannette was her sense that she was accomplishing little for the cause of peace. She quit her job before the end of the year.*

For about two years thereafter she took no active part in any peace movement but busied herself putting down roots at the Georgia farm, with intervals in Montana and in New York with Katharine Anthony. Along with millions of others all over the world, she searched the sky for favorable omens, drawing small comfort from either the foreign policy of the United States or the debates of the League of Nations in Geneva. In April

* She did not, however, resign from the League itself, retaining her membership all her life.

1927, however, a gleam of light appeared when Aristide Briand, French foreign minister, proposed that the United States and France sign a treaty renouncing war as an instrument of national policy. The following year Secretary of State Kellogg agreed to the proposal on condition that the principal powers in the world be co-signatories of the treaty and that the right of self-defense be reserved. The treaty was formally ratified in 1929 by France and the United States and was subsequently signed by sixty-three nations. Here at last was something for the peace advocates to get to work on, first to assure themselves of American commitment to the treaty, and next to plug the holes in the agreement whereby the country could be drawn into war regardless of solemn pledges.

As early as 1922 a Chicago lawyer named Salmon O. Levinson had proposed that peace activists throughout the United States center their efforts on obtaining a constitutional amendment to outlaw war, a plan that gained adherents slowly, gathering impetus only when the Kellogg-Briand Pact came up for discussion. The Women's Peace Union, a small but active group of pacifists, having decided that this was the most direct course to attain their ends, persuaded Senator Lynn J. Frazier of North Dakota to introduce a resolution in the Senate embodying Levinson's proposal. In April 1929 they invited Jeannette to come to Washington and lobby for the amendment in Congress. Ever since her resignation from her staff position on the Women's International League for Peace and Freedom Jeannette had been rusticating in Georgia—not quite idle, to be sure, for she had set up the Georgia Peace Society the year before—but conscious that Georgia was a backwater, out of the mainstream. "I have been in the country long enough to be quite thrilled with the idea of getting into the 'fight' again," she wrote in answer to this welcome invitation, and stated her terms. She would contract only for a stint of six months at $300 a month; she was willing to travel, but not extensively; she would not consent to do the usual "fieldwork."

Her six months with the Women's Peace Union was a period of intense activity on a par with her performance in the suffrage campaigns, as is shown in her report of May 25, giving a rundown of her meetings with various senators and congressmen. She had seen Senators Frazier, George of Georgia, Wheeler and

Walsh of Montana, Borah of Idaho, Norris of Nebraska, as well as Dill, Stephens and Deneen. All were friendly, some were brutally frank. Wheeler "thought the Peace Pact [the Kellogg-Briand Treaty] meant very little to the Senate. Seemed to fear that the administration is very militaristic and that nothing can be done. Very cynical about Public Opinion and its effect. Thinks there is little chance for any Peace Plan and no hope at all for the Amendment." Senator Borah she found very sympathetic, not opposed to the amendment. "However," she added, "this does not mean that he will go as far as we wish." Senator Norris did not favor the amendment; he thought it went too far and was discouraged about the length of time needed to get it passed. Senator LaFollette too thought the amendment as proposed went too far.

In the House she had called on LaGuardia, who seemed to be in a quandary; he was anxious to do something constructive for peace, but didn't know quite what that should be; meanwhile he would give serious consideration to the amendment. Jeannette's greatest disappointment came when she met with the women representatives, who seemed more strongly opposed than the men to an amendment to outlaw war; Mrs. Ruth Bryan Owen, for example, was very "militaristic"! (Some women evidently did not share Jeannette's concern for the future of the race.)

Jeannette did not limit her activities to lobbying in Congress, however; her fertile mind projected all sorts of schemes for involving the people more directly in the struggle for a permanent peace. In July she proposed that an intensive campaign to support the Frazier resolution be launched in several congressional districts where conditions were favorable, using such districts as "centers of infection," whence a peace epidemic might spread across the country. Later she suggested that the American Automobile Association initiate a propaganda drive urging the Federal government to spend more money on roads, the funds for which would be raised by reduced military expenditures. That these projects came to nothing is less important than that they show an ingenious mind at work on how to achieve political ends.

She had been expected to give some speeches in favor of the Frazier amendment, and at the end of the summer she gave her first talk on the radio, which had only recently come into use as a forum for the discussion of public affairs. At the prospect of addressing an unseen audience through the microphone she felt cold and scared, but "thrilled" all the same, as she wrote to the staff of the Women's Peace Union. Her talk over WEVD in New York on September 2, in which she called on the labor movement to back President Hoover's efforts at arms reduction, went off well and was favorably reviewed in the *New York Times*. In another radio talk she urged passage of the Frazier amendment because the Kellogg-Briand Pact did not offer a guaranty against American involvement in another war. The pact, she said, having been approved by the Senate, was part of the law of the land, but the Supreme Court held that "a treaty can be nullified by an Act of Congress of subsequent date insofar as the two are in conflict." In other words, a declaration of war by the Congress could not be held in violation of any treaty of peace unless Congress were enjoined by the Constitution from ever declaring war.

Jeannette stayed out the term of her engagement with the Women's Peace Union but did not seek to renew it. As early as May 25 she had written to Mrs. Mary B. Orr at the Union that even those senators and congressmen who were "most inclined to think our way are very doubtful as to our method of procedure." The method preferred by the Peace Union was to prepare speeches for congressmen to read or have inserted in the *Congressional Record*. Out of long experience Jeannette knew that such tactics were futile; that the best and only way to influence legislation was first to educate the people in the constituencies to the need for change, next to have the people put pressure on their representatives, and only then to try to persuade legislators to act. Her differences with the Peace Union were on the same basis as her differences with Alice Paul earlier: they did not have a "constituency," and they thought they could bring about change by working from the top down instead of from the bottom up, in democratic fashion.

In November 1929, therefore, she severed her connection with the Peace Union, but not before she had made arrangements to go on with her work for peace under other auspices. On October

Frederick J. Libby, chairman of the National Council for the Prevention of War.

4 she had written to Frederick J. Libby, chairman of the National Council for the Prevention of War:

> Dear Mr. Libby,
> You once told me to let you know when I was ready to do peace work. That was a long time ago. I hope you haven't forgotten it. The six months that the Women's Peace Union asked me to work with them will end the middle of November.

Libby was so pleased to have her collaboration that he offered her a place on his staff immediately, on her terms, assuring her of a certain freedom of action, since in his answering letter he granted that she wouldn't want to feel "muzzled." Evidently she had felt "muzzled" at the Women's Peace Union, an intolerable condition for so outspoken a creature as Jeannette Rankin.

The National Council for the Prevention of War, founded in 1921, was at this time the largest and most active group of peace advocates in the country. Libby, a Methodist minister who had given up his ministry for this purpose, had designed the NCPW as a kind of clearing house for the many existing peace societies, a central agency to provide programs and speakers locally while coordinating lobbying activities in the nation's capital. He worked tirelessly to bring churches, labor unions, farmers' groups and even businessmen's associations into the peace movement. To man his office he had assembled a force of dedicated assistants, many of whom toiled with missionary fervor for little or no pay, organizing meetings and demostrations out in the field or gathering material for propaganda issued from the Washington headquarters. Funds were perennially low, sometimes nonexistent, and in such emergencies Libby would search out some sympathetic philanthropist or solicit money from more affluent societies. Devoted though he was to peace, however, there was a naïve strain in Libby that blinded him to fundamental political and economic realities, except in the most general terms. He thought he was doing God's work and that the Lord would provide; the Lord would open the eyes of men to the wickedness of war. A gentle man, he was easily taken in by pious expressions of peaceful aims by a corporation lawyer like John Foster Dulles or members of the America First Committee.

Jeannette was to remain with the National Council for the Prevention of War for the next nine years as a lobbyist and propagandist for peace, the quest for which had become the dominant motive in her life. No less dedicated than Libby to the cause, she was far more realistic, having learned in a hard school to pursue that which was possible in the realm of politics. She would work with the National Council, but in her own way, starting at the bottom, with the people. She had already, in fact, begun to build up a constituency for peace in Georgia, which for some years to come would share her interest with the peace program in the nation.

VIII

The People Want Peace

In Georgia, Jeannette told herself, she had at last the nucleus of a constituency for peace. Already in February 1928, along with some of the faculty of the University of Georgia and other intellectuals in the area of Athens, she had set up the Georgia Peace Society, of which she became the secretary and guiding spirit. Within a few weeks of its birth the society completed arrangements for holding a statewide Conference on the Cause and Cure of War, the first of three such meetings convened to make a study of American foreign policy and gather support for a disarmament program. The emergence of the Georgia Peace Society seemed so promising that Libby, possibly at Jeannette's suggestion, contemplated opening a branch office of the National Council for the Prevention of War in Atlanta.

As the most active member of the Peace Society, Jeannette was able to put all her experience as well as her theories of political action to the test by launching campaigns in the districts against naval expansion and the ROTC, or in favor of the Frazier amendment, for example. Back in 1925, when she was working for the Women's International League for Peace and Freedom, she had conceived the idea of "a center of infection" of peace sentiment; Georgia, she now thought, could be such a center. While it is true that some of her notions of how to arouse interest were old-fashioned, as in schemes for holding parades in county seats, she made a very real contribution in her organization of local groups, in her repeated speaking tours to educate the electorate, and in her continual injunctions to the voters to make their views known to their representatives. Georgia had never known anyone quite like her.

Her deal with Libby gave her more latitude than she had enjoyed when working with the other peace societies. This was evidently the point of her stipulation that she should not be "muzzled" during her association with the National Council for the Prevention of War. During the period from 1910 to 1919 she had had a sense of great accomplishment, of sharing in and forwarding great social reforms, of using her talents to the fullest extent. In the twenties these talents had been used only sporadically and to little effect, throttling the energy by which she was driven. When she joined the National Council she entered into a period of almost constant activity for more than a decade, joining in the common cause with her associates but also taking independent action when she thought it would bring results.

Although the National Council did not open a branch office in Atlanta, Jeannette seized the first opportunity that presented itself to bring Georgia into the forefront of the peace movement. After the Kellogg-Briand Pact was ratified by the Senate in 1929, she gave a speech before the National Education Association, which was then holding its annual meeting in Atlanta, urging its members to support the Frazier Amendment to outlaw war. While she was in the state capitol, it occurred to her to place the issue before the legislature as well. She found two state representatives who fell in with her scheme; they obligingly offered a resolution to petition Congress to outlaw war by constitutional amendment. Granted the privilege of addressing the legislature on the resolution, Jeannette spoke with such earnestness that questions from the floor seemed to her quite friendly, even sympathetic. "Do you think they're going to pass it?" she whispered to Speaker Richard Russell (later United States senator), who had invited her to sit beside him on the platform. "If I thought so I'd go right down and stop them!" Russell replied crisply. In effect he took no chances but promptly had a substitute resolution introduced condemning the Frazier amendment, which was passed with dispatch by his well-trained henchmen. Jeannette was not cast down by this, feeling that a point had been won in that the question had been debated at all.

In February 1930 she took part in the third and final Conference on the Cause and Cure of War held by the Georgia Peace Society, at which she conducted a forum on how women could help shape public opinion and influence the legislative process. The most useful function they could perform, she told her group, was to "keep up a continuous barrage of letters to the President, the Senators, and Members of Congress." Over the years, whatever the age or sex of her audience, she always stressed this method for the advancement of any cause she championed.

> If you don't like what your representative is doing or failing to do [she would say] write him a letter asking his position on a certain issue. If he doesn't reply, or if his answer is unsatisfactory, or if it is written by one of his secretaries, write him another letter, and another, and another, until he begins to take you seriously and responds to the point.

And then she would add with a smile: "I do not advise you to write him more than once a week."*

In addition to her forum at the Conference on the Cause and Cure of War, she carried on one of her typical barnstorming campaigns, talking to students' groups and women's clubs and turning up at newspaper offices to make sure the proceedings got the proper coverage. When it was over she wrote to Libby that she was "tired but happy," a sign that she had found responsive audiences.

One of the resolutions passed by the Conference on the Cause and Cure of War was especially gratifying to Jeannette: it urged that no more battleships be added to the United States Navy, and that other reductions in the fleet be made in accordance with the terms of the treaty negotiated by Secretary of State Stimson

* Although she herself never lost faith in this method, she confessed that in her own case it sometimes miscarried. One Georgia congressman paid no attention to her repeated inquiries for many months, at the end of which he sent her a government publication containing a list of cookbooks! But she knew that her method was correct because in several significant cases it brought the desired results.

with the British and the Japanese at the London Naval Conference. Since her first assignment for the National Council for the Prevention of War had been to lobby in Congress in favor of ratification of this treaty, her work in Georgia dovetailed nicely with her activities in Washington. The treaty, ratified by Congress in July 1930, extended the capital ship "holiday" until 1936, along with limitations on the total tonnage of cruisers, destroyers and submarines.

The peace advocates rejoiced at this victory, which had been won only after President Hoover had called a special session of the Congress and forced the measure through the Senate during a heat wave, but the big-navy men, though outvoted for the moment, had no intention of giving up the ship. Among these was a Georgia congressman, Carl Vinson, who was the ranking Democrat on the House Naval Affairs Committee in 1930 and chairman of the committee the following year. In 1931 Vinson introduced in the House a naval expansion bill to cost $616,000,000, in direct violation of the spirit of the London Naval Conference, the first thrust of the militarists to reverse the direction toward international disarmament.

On learning of this bill Jeannette at once decided to counterattack. Rallying the peace forces in Georgia, she went into Vinson's district with her followers to inform his constituents about the measure and in what way it was a threat to peace. Within a short time Vinson's office was deluged with letters and telegrams opposing his plans to expand the navy, an opposition so unexpected and so formidable that he thought it best not to call for a vote on his bill, and did not report out a bill passed by the Senate along the same lines, calling for an even larger appropriation. Jeannette's letter-writing campaign had had immediate consequences. For the moment Vinson was blocked in his designs, but it was far from a knockout blow, as he was no political amateur.

And so the decade of the thirties began for Jeannette with a spate of work, as the people of the United States who for the past ten years had shown their revulsion against wars and against involvement in the disputes of other nations once more were called upon to make positive decisions or be led into combat through ignorance. Peace advocates spoke for the larger, less articulate majority, they estimated; their opponents included those for whom unquestioned acceptance of their government's military actions was a matter of principle (my country, right or wrong), as well as others for whom patriotism was a business affair: army and navy professionals, bankers, manufacturers of armaments, and their dependents, hirelings, and subsidiaries.

Along with other peace societies, the National Council divided its efforts among campaigns of education, of support for international agreements and organizations to resolve or arbitrate differences between nations, and attempts to prevent the United States from being drawn into disputes anywhere around the world. Jeannette was deeply and emotionally involved in all of this, beginning with her support of the naval limitation treaty and her opposition to the Vinson bill. In 1931 she campaigned for United States membership in the World Court (Permanent Court of International Justice at The Hague), which had been set up in 1922 as an instrument to settle international disputes and which was deemed superior for that purpose to the League of Nations. She appeared before a House committee and called on many senators to present arguments in favor of America's joining the Court. She argued in vain. Senators Borah of Idaho and Johnson of California, powerful members of the Foreign Relations Committee, were strongly opposed; the Hearst press across the country thundered against it; and Father Coughlin filled the airwaves with warnings of dire consequences should the United States take part in such an alliance. The measure hung fire for some years and was finally defeated in 1935.

Between spells of lobbying in Washington and coursing through Georgia, Jeannette embarked from time to time on speaking tours elsewhere, exhibiting as much steam power as if she were running for high office. One typical program in Pittsburgh in November 1930 consisted of two talks on Sunday, one at the Friends Meeting at eleven in the morning and the other at the Presbyterian Church at six in the evening; a visit to the Teachers Training School on Monday, with talks at 10:15, noon, 12:30 and 5:45 P.M. before different groups; a radio address on Tuesday as well as a talk to young people at the Baptist Church at 6:30; ending with a speech at the University of Pittsburgh on Wednesday.

By the summer of 1931, after such exertions, Jeannette was ready for a holiday. She went to Europe, but here too she combined work with pleasure, for her destination was Geneva, where she represented the National Council in preliminary arrangements for the disarmament conference which was to be held the following year. Her observation of the sittings at the League of Nations on this occasion confirmed a belief she had held since it was first set up: that the League was neither constituted for nor dedicated to preventing wars. In a report to Libby she wrote that its proceedings reminded her of games she had played in her childhood: "When we were lost in our fantasies and wished to come back to reality or interrupt the game, we called 'King's Ex.' " The rest of her European trip was more pleasurable, but the fearful pace of her work earlier had taken its toll, for on her return from Paris she went into a hospital for an operation.

Meanwhile the first tremors of the Great Depression were beginning to be felt throughout the country, radiating out from the stock market crash of October 1929 to the breadlines of 1932. As the crisis deepened, vital issues, both economic and social, confronted a nation unprepared by a decade of phony prosperity for mature judgments on domestic problems, let alone foreign affairs. When the two national party conventions met in Chicago in June 1932 to name the man to head each ticket, their delegates were concerned less with how to prevent wars than with how to prevent a domestic debacle. The peace advocates, however, clung to their basic premise that all social questions could be dealt with intelligently given a worldwide renunciation of war. They therefore descended on Chicago in large numbers to demand a peace plank in the platforms of both parties.*

The Peace March on Chicago in the summer of 1932 was conceived and organized by Jeannette with Florence Boeckel of the National Council for the Prevention of War; it was a paradigm of the peace marches of more recent years in protest against the

* Forty years later it is difficult to dismiss the peace advocates as impractical idealists, for a good number of economists and historians are agreed that despite all the ameliorative measures of the New Deal and succeeding administrations, the underlying weaknesses of the American economic system have been mitigated only by war, the preparation for war, and the cold war.

Beside the lead car in a motorcade from Washington to Chicago in 1932 to urge the Republican and Democratic national conventions to adopt a peace plank.

Wide World Photos

war in Southeast Asia. On June 2 Jeannette led off in the first car from Washington. Dressed in a fetching summer costume, a flared print dress with a trim jacket, a becoming hat, strap pumps and white gloves, she posed for the photographers wearing a broad smile—the smile that brought out the quaint tilt of her eyes and brows. In Chicago the Washington delegation met with groups from widely scattered parts of the country: Georgia, Kentucky, Massachusetts, Maine, California and Oregon, including young people who had hitchhiked or ridden the rails to arrive at the rendezvous. One young man came from Oregon by freight train, dressed in overalls "to qualify him to hobnob with the hoboes," as Frederick Libby put it, "carrying his street clothes wrapped in a bundle under his arm."

Before the official opening of each convention the peace groups held a great parade consisting of more than 700 automobiles, according to one account, with banners flying and placards on display. Prominent in the motorcade were "double casualties," men disabled in World War I who were also unemployed. Newspaper and radio coverage of the event was very friendly, one commentator describing the first procession as "the sweetest thing in the Republican Convention." The young people in 1932 were warmly received in Chicago, where thirty-six years later youths on another peace mission would be met with tear gas and night sticks. At a dinner at Hull House Jane Addams welcomed the young adherents to the peace movement; she said she was very happy "to see somebody besides old ladies at peace meetings," because "if there is to be another fight among the nations, it will be their war. . . ."

Miss Addams appeared as the first witness to urge a peace plank before the resolutions committees of both parties, but neither party adopted it. When Jeannette realized that her associates were making no headway with either the Republicans or the Democrats, she pleaded with Libby to form a National Peace Party, not so much in the hope of supplanting either of the old established political machines as in the belief that a party such as she recommended would rally all the peace advocates under one banner and give them some leverage in political decisions. Libby, however, begged off, saying that he did not have the funds for such a scheme.

Jeannette did not believe that the pacifists could take much comfort in the nomination and election of Franklin Roosevelt; neither did she share the views of those liberals who looked on him uncritically, remembering his antisuffrage stand in 1912 as well as his indifference to the evils of child labor. Nevertheless, as the New Deal measures to stem the effects of the Great Depression were brought forward, she withheld judgment on his ultimate aims, for in her travels she had had ample opportunity to see the privation and suffering among the people throughout the country.

But even the sight of such misery did not deflect her from her primary purpose. Throughout 1932 and 1933 she concentrated her efforts on winning support for the Geneva Disarmament Conference, which was designed, like the London Naval Conference, to reverse the trend toward an arms race. In 1932 President Hoover set before the Geneva Conference a plan to abolish all bombing planes and tanks, and to reduce all land and naval forces by about thirty percent; after his election President Roosevelt also supported general multilateral disarmament, though halfheartedly. But the Japanese invasion of Manchuria in 1932 and Hitler's accession to power in Germany in 1933 led to fatal divisions among the delegates to the conference, Britain and France holding out against any further disarmament despite the willingness of the majority to go along with the American proposals. On October 26, 1933, Jeannette wrote to Libby in a mood of great discouragement:

> I am feeling very much let down; after making twenty-two speeches and driving the car over a thousand miles, getting more than sixty resolutions with every congressional district in Georgia represented, and spending one whole night catching a train, then to have England and France acting like stupid children. . . . Roosevelt decides to build tanks and airplanes while the Disarmament Conference is still struggling.

The phrase "spending one whole night catching a train" strikes one as particularly touching; we are inclined to be outraged by some personal inconvenience when grieving over truly cosmic disasters.

But her disappointment with the failure of the Disarmament Conference did not dampen her spirits for long. She felt that she had not misjudged the strong current of antiwar sentiment among the American people; it was there, and it was not politically impotent. In 1934 a Senate investigating committee under the chairmanship of Senator Gerald P. Nye of North Dakota undertook its famous inquiry into the munitions makers in World War I. The usefulness of such a committee depends not only on the earnestness of its members but in equal measure on the intelligence and skill of its staff, and Jeannette was one of several persons instrumental in having Stephen Raushenbush, a brilliant liberal lawyer formerly associated with the American

Civil Liberties Union, appointed secretary. She interviewed Senators George, Pope, and Barbour, who were serving on the Nye Committee, to urge that Raushenbush be retained as their counsel. Members of the committee staff still speak of her keen interest in their work, her faithful attendance at the hearings, and her readiness to help them in areas where she was informed.

She also spread word of the Nye Committee revelations in Georgia, speaking over the radio in Athens and devising for peace booths at the county fairs such slogans as: "All they that taketh the sword shall perish by taxes," and "You can no more win a war than you can win an earthquake." In the fall of 1934 she also began to campaign against compulsory military training (the ROTC) in Georgia schools and colleges, an undertaking on which she spent some years without success. Her work that fall was particularly arduous, since she had no secretary and no telephone and received no money from the National Council for her activities in Georgia. Like everyone else at the time, the National Council was in straitened circumstances and had long been in arrears on her salary; since Libby could not even reimburse her for her traveling expenses and mailing costs, he once recommended that on her trips she "live off the country."

In the course of her pacific march through Georgia that fall she was invited to give a series of three lectures on disarmament at Brenau College in Gainesville, one of the most expensive and conservative women's colleges in the state, whose acting president, Dr. Pearce, suggested that these talks might be preliminary to her assumption of a "Chair of Peace." The offer was made informally, but not frivolously, since Brenau issued a press release concerning the offer. In any case no salary was mentioned for the moment, and the chair could not be established until funds were raised to pay for it, an unlikely occurrence during the Depression. But professional patriots immediately sprang into action: American Legion Post Number One in Atlanta sounded the alarm, denouncing the plan for a "Chair of Peace" as "Un-American," "communistic," and a threat to the nation's preparedness. Jeannette was described in this blast as a "radical pacifist" and a member of such "subversive" organizations as the National Council for the Prevention of War and the American Civil Liberties Union! Barring the pejorative implications of these charges, none save one could be denied, and in answer to that Jeannette wrote to Dr. Pearce:

> I come of seventeenth-century American stock. I have never subscribed to the doctrines of communism. . . . I am first and last an American citizen, believing wholeheartedly in the fundamental doctrines upon which the American government is founded.

Somewhat later she said that "the sum of my reputed radicalism seems to be my opposition to war, to competitive armaments and to predatory interests." This was of course precisely what made her a subversive character in the eyes of the Legionnaires. The truth is that she was aggressive and pertinacious as a pacifist, a person to be reckoned with.

Still there is no question that Jeannette was distressed by the attacks made on her, although she had the satisfaction of learning that the trustees of Brenau College were not backing down but were continuing their attempts to raise $150,000 to endow the Chair of Peace. But the American Legion did not call off the campaign of vilification. In the autumn of 1935, just as she was beginning to organize a conference on peace in Sandersville, a series of anonymous letters stating that the National Council for the Prevention of War was being run by Communists began to appear here and there, and on October 10 the *Macon Evening Journal* published an article by a Legionnaire containing charges so defamatory that they could not go unanswered. Jeannette Rankin, the article read, had been "branded in the courts of Atlanta as a rank Communist"; moreover, she had been fired from "one of the South's finest schools for forming a so-called chair of peace and for advocating Communist ideas."

To put an end to this persecution Jeannette decided to sue the newspaper for libel, but where would she find the money to institute a suit? The National Council was as usual in arrears on her salary, and at this particular moment her poverty was more of an embarrassment than ever. On October 14 she wrote to Libby from Sandersville: "With the American Legion after me, I cannot leave here without paying my bills." Libby sent her enough to get her out of town with honor, and then went even further; he got the National Council to put up $500 for legal fees in her suit against the *Macon Evening Journal.**

As is common in libel suits, Jeannette asked for damages of $50,000 to begin with, but on advice of her counsel, after negotiations that ran on for more than a year, agreed to a settlement out of court amounting to $1,000, along with a retraction. On November 16, 1936, the front page of the *Macon Evening Journal* carried a handsome apology for the libelous article, stating that Jeannette was "held in the highest esteem for the sincerity of her efforts," and that she had "an international reputation as a pacifist." The paper claimed that it disagreed with her only on the question of disarmament. Often in the years that followed, when speaking before groups that had trouble raising money for peace propaganda, Jeannette would describe the incident, ending up with, "and they gave me $1,000 and said I was a nice lady." Granted that the money was very welcome, it was a distasteful way to replenish one's bank account. Though the *Macon Evening Journal* recanted, the American Legion continued to assail her in its publications; the next year Legionnaires as far away as Providence, Rhode Island, charged that Libby and Rankin were Communists, Libby secretly and Jeannette openly.

Meanwhile Raushenbush and his team of investigators for the Nye Committee had produced witnesses and testimony that proved beyond a doubt that the concerted activities of the "merchants of death," the bankers, and Allied propagandists had been of decisive influence in bringing about America's entrance into World War I. As one damaging disclosure after another

* An interesting sidelight on the affair is that the National Council put up the money only after making a fruitless appeal to the American Civil Liberties Union for financial aid in the suit. The newspaper article in question had cited as proof of Jeannette's membership in the Communist party the fact that she was listed as a vice president of the American Civil Liberties Union. Not long before this, Angelo Herndon, a black radical, had been convicted of subversive activities in Georgia, and it was known that material issued by the American Civil Liberties Union had been found among his effects when he was arrested. Herndon's conviction was reversed by the highest court in Georgia, and on appeal by the United States Supreme Court, but these decisions had no weight with the professional patriots. The American Civil Liberties Union, however, refused to be associated with Jeannette's suit, its counsel, Morris Ernst, taking the position that there should be the widest latitude in publishing, even of "untrue statements in the press."

broke into the news, the reaction all over the country was one of astonishment: How could we have been so misled, so deceived? And then the corollary: How can we prevent a repetition of such tragic involvements?

One of those who came up with an answer to this last question was Representative Louis L. Ludlow of Indiana, who offered a resolution in the House calling for a constitutional amendment to prevent Congress from declaring war without first submitting the matter to a popular referendum, except in case of invasion. Jeannette lobbied for this resolution in 1935 and appeared before the House Judiciary Committee to argue for its passage. The Judiciary Committee held the resolution locked up for two years until it was discharged on petition of a majority of the representatives; it finally came to a vote on January 10, 1938, and was defeated by a small margin, under administration pressure.

Another reaction to the Nye Committee investigation was expressed in the McSwain resolution, which was ostensibly designed to take the profits out of war. Jeannette was suspicious of this proposal and denounced it as "a rich man's scheme to fool the people." She went before the House Military Affairs Committee in January 1935 to offer a substitute plan to take the profits out of war. It was an ingenious project, based on the premise that munitions makers and bankers were not alone in profiting from war; almost all civilians had a stake in it. After many attempts to bring the trade unions into the peace movement, she had once remarked, for example, that "the men at the head of the AFL are not nearly as anxious for peace as they are for jobs, and often peace programs conflict with what seems to be their individual economic interest (war profits)." On a declaration of war, she now proposed to the Military Affairs Committee, let all money and credit be replaced for the duration with fiat bills equal to what they replaced, the "frozen" prewar dollars or credits to be restored at the end of hostilities. Since the fiat money would then be declared worthless, profiteering would be eliminated. There must have been a mischievous glint in her eye when she added:

> You should pay $30 a month, or whatever a soldier's wage is, in whatever currency is used, to everyone, and let everyone have

> a tin cup and bread card and subsist on the same food that the soldier does, beginning with the President. For members of Congress who have voted for war [let them receive], not only the $30 a month but also the honor of carrying the flag in battle, so that they would feel that they are doing their bit.

Such plain speaking and unorthodox economics did not appeal to certain congressmen (perhaps most of them), who failed to see the humor in it and did not enjoy having their patriotic motives called into question in this irreverent manner.

A more hopeful consequence of the Nye Committee disclosures was the growing sentiment in Congress for a neutrality bill that would prevent American involvement in foreign wars by prohibiting the sale or transport of war materials to any of the parties so engaged. Mussolini's unprovoked assault on Ethiopia, which it was feared might draw other nations into the conflict—as Austria-Hungary's attack on Serbia had done some twenty years earlier—lent urgency to the need for *mandatory* neutrality legislation. It was because of seizures and sinkings of American merchant vessels from 1915 to 1917 that the United States had entered World War I as a combatant, and future entanglements could only be avoided, the peace advocates believed, if traffic with any countries at war were outlawed. Under the sponsorship of Senators Nye, Clark, Vandenberg and Bone, a mandatory neutrality bill was introduced in the Senate in the summer of 1935 and passed without opposition. A similar bill in the House, sponsored by Congressman Wright of Ohio, was blocked in the Foreign Affairs Committee because of pressure from the White House. Roosevelt wanted to substitute a bill giving him *discretionary* powers to limit our shipping to combatants, and McReynolds of Tennessee, chairman of the Foreign Affairs Committee, shared the president's views. McReynolds would not allow the Wright bill to be discharged from the committee.

This was the situation when Jeannette came up from Georgia on August 19 to lead the fight for mandatory neutrality legislation on behalf of the National Council for the Prevention of War. She launched her campaign by writing 175 personal letters to congressmen asking them to petition for release of the bill, but this could not be effected before the House recessed. If she wanted the mandatory measure to pass before the end of the session, Jeannette realized that she had to work fast. The main obstacle to its passage, as she saw it, was McReynolds, and she resolved to fight him on his home territory, in his Tennessee district, as she had fought Vinson. This operation, carried on for twelve grueling days in the heat of the summer, was her greatest single achievement in the thirties, justifying her faith in participatory democracy, in educating the people to educate their representatives.

It was another of her one-man campaigns, but it was conducted with more speed and even greater precision than her earlier battles. An old suffrage friend, Abby Crawford Milton, who lived in Chattanooga, the largest city in McReynolds's district, offered Jeannette a base of operations and organization assistance. Mrs. Milton arranged a speaking program covering ten counties that ran for twelve hours a day almost without interruption, in talks before school assemblies, church groups, women's clubs and other societies, ending up at nine o'clock in the evening, as a rule, with a radio address. (One of the places where Jeannette spoke that summer was the room where Scopes had been tried for teaching evolution in the schools a decade earlier.) With such a crowded schedule she had little time for lunch or dinner en route, so Mrs. Milton thoughtfully provided her with an enormous breakfast in bed every morning, a meal consisting of steak, potatoes, green vegetables, pie and coffee—fuel for a whole day's touring and stump speaking.

Jeannette's approach to the people of Tennessee began with a disarming plea for assistance to a poor, helpless (!) woman: she came from Montana, she said, a state which had no influence in Congress, while Tennessee was represented in Washington by the Speaker of the House of Representatives, Secretary of State Hull, and the chairman of the House Foreign Affairs Committee. Would her listeners please write to Congressman McReynolds and urge him to vote for a mandatory neutrality bill to keep the United States out of foreign wars? Her appeal must have been compelling, for letters began pouring into the office of McReynolds, who was not accustomed to so much attention from his constituents. "He thought they would never know how he voted," Jeannette said afterward. "He learned."

Like Vinson, McReynolds was taken aback by the volume and fervor of the messages from his district, and began to waver in his opposition to the Neutrality Bill. When Congress reconvened Jeannette and Warren Mullin of the National Council posted themselves on either side of the door of the House chamber as the congressmen emerged after the roll call, asking each man and woman to inquire of McReynolds when he would allow a vote on the bill. The response was heartening. Jeannette thought of still another stratagem: Passing through the Foreign Affairs Committee room, she suggested in a whisper to Congressman Wright that the measure be made effective for six months, instead of a year. This clinched it. McReynolds at last gave way and cleared the path for a vote in the House, where it passed by a decisive majority.

Jeannette always sought means to dramatize the peace movement and give it a positive aspect; when the National Council, for example, was at a loss for a suitable name for its bulletin, she suggested *Peace Action* to convey the notion of an affirmative movement. The periodical appeared under that title until the Council itself folded. On another occasion she called for someone to write a comedy on a war theme. "People must laugh at war to get over their tenseness," she wrote to Warren Mullin. (Was she thinking of *Lysistrata* or *What Price Glory?*) In 1935 she conceived the idea of celebrating the stand of those members of Congress who had opposed our entrance into World War I. The ceremony took place in Statuary Hall at the Capitol on April 6—the anniversary of the declaration of war—where tribute was paid to all fifty-six dissidents, and wreaths were laid at the base of the statues of Champ Clark and Robert LaFollette. Jeannette reserved for herself the privilege of honoring Claude Kitchin, who had spoken that memorable phrase: "It takes neither moral nor physical courage to declare a war for others to fight."

Throughout the whole of 1935 Jeannette worked at high pressure, throwing herself into one project after another without a stop, a state of affairs that suited her temperament admirably and almost served to make her forget her money problems. One former employee in the office of the National Council says that Libby assumed that Jeannette had an adequate private income, or could draw on her brother Wellington when she ran short, but she was always reluctant to do this. The Council's funds—from member groups and an occasional gift from a sympathetic millionaire—were very uneven and highly unreliable, to such a point that in 1935 Libby started a million-dollar bond drive to give the peace movement a solid base. Jeannette was photographed as she sold the first bond to Senator Nye, but the whole scheme was unrealistic and quickly fell through when Libby discovered that he lacked money even to print the bond certificates.

Jeannette's financial situation became more acute in 1935 when her little house in Bogart burned. In 1933 she had planned some additions to the dwelling, writing to Libby that she was "adding a house to my room" and confessing that there was nothing more time-consuming and at the same time more amusing than building. Rather than rebuild the house in Bogart, however, she sold the land and bought a cottage and thirty-three acres in Watkinsville, ten miles away, for which she had to pay all of $300. The new place, however, needed repairs, additions and equipment to make it livable, all of which was a further drain on her meager resources. At a low point that year she wrote Libby a letter of entreaty: "Am living in true Georgia fashion. No money. The stores are 'furnishing' me with food and gas. They say, 'It's so long since we've had any money we done got used to it.' " On another occasion, when she was called to Washington, she wrote: "I'll not be able to leave Georgia until I have some money. My debts are almost $200. Some I can hold off but others I can't." In answer to these piteous appeals Libby would send her small sums from time to time, never quite catching up with what the Council owed her, and never arranging matters on a businesslike basis. It was not until the end of the following year that the settlement of the libel suit against the *Macon Evening Journal* brought her some relief.

By 1936 the outlook for world peace had grown murky; armed conflicts were raging in the Far East, where Japan was extending her war against China; in Africa, where Mussolini was completing his conquest of Ethiopia; and now in Europe, where the Spanish Falangists were engaged in civil war against the

Republican government. In the face of this rising threat American peace groups—the Quakers, the Women's International League for Peace and Freedom, the Fellowship of Reconciliation, and the National Council for the Prevention of War—decided to join forces in an Emergency Peace Campaign, a nationwide drive to dramatize and publicize the growing crisis. George Lansbury, the British M.P., a leading pacifist, came over from England in April to launch the campaign at a dinner in Washington, to which Eleanor Roosevelt sent a letter of friendly greeting. Lansbury on this occasion made a proposal that struck at the underlying causes of current international tensions: namely, that a world conference be called to negotiate equalization of resources among the have and have-not nations. Such equalization, in his view, would put an end to Fascist aggression and remove the causes of war. It was a solution that had a strong appeal for many pacifists right up to the outbreak of World War II, and one to which Jeannette subscribed without reserve. (When Lansbury put his suggestion before Franklin Roosevelt, however, the president received it with some caution and said he would need a "peg" to hang it on.)

Jeannette took an active part in the Emergency Peace Campaign, particularly in Georgia. She drew up plans for a children's peace parade, designing the flags and banners to be carried, the costumes to be worn, the order of march, all down to the last detail. Again she went on a speaking tour, telling her audiences that the threat of war was very real and that Armistice Day, November 11, commemorated only "the temporary cessation of hostilities" in 1918. She urged her hearers not to accept wars as inevitable: "The fact that we have never had peace need not deter us. Every day we see things we have never seen before. . . . There was a time when cannibalism, parricide and dueling were not even against the law. War can likewise be outgrown." In a warning against the temptation of fighting a "Holy War" against a wicked enemy, she drew on her fund of funny stories, telling of the little boy in Sunday School who couldn't wait for the teacher to let him give an account of his good deed of the week. When his chance to speak came he said he had seen a big boy jump on a little boy, so he had taken an axe and split the bully's head open. In another vein she denied that she was an isolationist, maintaining that like Franklin Roosevelt she was an isolationist only against war, using his very words.

She had been hopeful that the peace movement would take root in Georgia and spread out from there all over the country, but attacks against her and other peace advocates were being mounted steadily by the local American Legion. The groups of youths—trained by Jeannette—who went out to the rural areas in many states during the Emergency Peace Campaign met with a very unpleasant reception in Georgia, where they were "hounded," as they said, by Legionnaires who had been alerted by the Brenau College incident to sniff out "peacemongers." Even the Georgia Peace Society was declining in numbers, some members charging that Jeannette was dictatorial. What is more likely is that the fainthearted were dismayed by her singleness of purpose and the unfavorable publicity she had provoked. Perhaps aware of her declining influence, she took it upon herself to make one more bold stroke to revive the state's peace forces.

Her old adversary, Representative Carl Vinson, was coming up for reelection in 1936 to a seat in which he was well entrenched; nevertheless, she would try to have him defeated. It will be remembered that in 1931 she had discouraged him from reporting out a naval expansion bill by inciting his constituents to deluge him with letters opposing the measure. Vinson had simply bided his time and in 1933 had introduced a similar bill, calling for an even larger appropriation this time. Jeannette learned that the Vinson-Trammel Bill, as it was called, had the secret support of President Franklin Roosevelt, who, like his kinsman, Theodore Roosevelt, subscribed to the theory that whatever nation ruled the waves ruled the world. The Vinson-Trammel Bill eventually passed both Houses and was signed by the President in 1934, and further increases in the navy were to come as the war approached. Jeannette now undertook to have Vinson repudiated at the polls.

It was perhaps her success in defeating McReynolds's obstructive tactics with regard to the Neutrality Act in 1935 that made her overconfident in this encounter. In the summer of 1936 she went on the campaign trail, speaking in high schools, at prayer meetings, at women's clubs, indoors and at outdoor assemblies in Vinson's district in an effort to persuade the voters that he was an undesirable candidate. She even went so far as to try to persuade someone to stand against Vinson in the primaries, offering to provide funds for the contest. To her dismay, these tactics had exactly the opposite effect of what she intended. Up to this time Vinson had felt so secure in his seat that he never bothered to campaign actively to retain it; now under the threat of Jeannette's assault he was obliged to go before the electorate and woo their support. Moreover, he commanded ample campaign funds and a well-oiled political machine. To no one's surprise he won by a handsome margin, gaining 10,000 more votes than in 1934. When the primary returns came in (in Georgia at that time a victory in the Democratic primaries was equivalent to election) Jeannette admitted that she felt "flatter than a pancake." She had been instrumental in getting out the vote, and the voters had made their choice!

Meanwhile she had the satisfaction of seeing the Neutrality Act of 1935 renewed at the end of February 1936 for a year. Although the measure was supposed to operate in the case of wars between nations, and not in the case of insurrections, the administration, under pressure from religious and conservative groups, chose to apply its terms to the civil war in Spain. From the beginning of the Spanish war the rebel forces received arms and other assistance from Fascist Italy and Nazi Germany, while the legally constituted Republican government was denied aid from France and England, and only later got help from the Soviet Union. It was because of this unequal situation, so heavily weighted against a democracy, that Socialists like Norman Thomas and many other liberal, peace-loving Americans urged that the Embargo Act should not be held applicable in the Spanish civil war. Jeannette was not of this opinion; neither she nor the President foresaw that the triumph of fascism in Spain was to give the Axis powers reason to believe that the democracies would not stand up to them anywhere in the world.

With no intention of aiding the Spanish Republicans, the administration in 1937 pressed for modification of the Neutrality Act to give the President discretionary powers in its application. Jeannette returned to Washington to fight for retention of the mandatory clause of the act and on February 16 appeared before the House Foreign Affairs Committee, prepared to make a strong presentation. But she found the going tougher than before. The committee's chairman, McReynolds, was still smarting from the wounds she had inflicted on his self-esteem in 1935 when he was compelled to release the first Neutrality bill for a vote. He greeted her with some asperity:

> I understand, Miss Rankin, you have been taking quite an active part in this . . . legislation. . . . I understand further that you have been trying to assist in arranging a meeting with members of Congress . . . not on this committee, and it appeared to [me] as if you were trying not to cooperate . . . but on the contrary to block the committee. How about that?

"Mr. Chairman," Jeannette replied, "at the request of several members of Congress, I announced there was going to be a meeting. However, I did not make any arrangements for it, except as requested."

"Are you what may be called a lobbyist?" asked McReynolds. Jeannette saw nothing shameful in the title.

> Yes, sir, I am a professional lobbyist. . . . I began lobbying in 1913 for woman suffrage. I lobbied in 1915 . . . and in the early twenties I worked for the Child Labor Amendment. . . . There was a period when I thought there was no use of lobbying, that the people were not ready for peace. . . . [But] when the Kellogg pact went into effect, I felt that since the Government had given its solemn word they would not settle disputes by war, there would be fertile ground to work on. Mr. Libby asked me to work in Congress. I might state here that if it were not for Mr. Libby I would do exactly the same work on my own initiative. . . . I do not feel . . . that I was not cooperating with the committee. . . . The more discussion the clearer our opinion becomes.

McReynolds had the last word, however. "This committee," he said, "has always tried to give everyone a hearing . . . but we are amazed when an effort is made to organize another committee by a lobbyist. . . . We do not appreciate it." And he dismissed her.

Ignoring the frantic pleas of the antiwar activists as well as public opinion polls that indicated a desire for even stricter neutrality legislation, Congress passed the Neutrality Act of 1937 substantially in the form urged by the President. In a reversal of the policy expressed in the two earlier measures, the new act granted him the power to add anything he wished to the list of goods carried by American ships to warring countries. This not only would permit him to favor one side or another, but could be interpreted to mean that in selected cases he need take no action at all. In effect it relinquished American claims to freedom of the seas. During the summer of 1937, when Japan went to war with China without a formal declaration, Roosevelt placed no restrictions on supplies flowing to either country from American sources, although the Spanish embargo was still rigidly maintained!

Jeannette saw the direction taken by the administration as leading on a direct course to involvement in the wars of other nations; moreover, Congress was showing ever greater inclination to bow to the will of the President in this explosive area. But the people were on her side, she believed fervently; therefore she would go out once more and tell them what was happening and what was at stake. During the first six months of 1937 she gave ninety-three speeches in ten states and the District of Columbia, addressing in all more than 20,000 citizens in addition to the radio audiences. She was well received by those within reach of her voice—the already converted?—but a powerful current of feeling was rising in many segments of the population that the rapacity of the Germans, the Italians and the Japanese could not be checked without a confrontation of the great powers sooner or later.

One day in June she went to call on Eleanor Roosevelt at the White House to plead for curbs on military spending; having once taken part in a radio symposium with Mrs. Roosevelt during the Emergency Peace Campaign, she hoped that the President's wife would share her anxieties and try to turn Roosevelt away from the course that was leading to war. In her newspaper column the following day, however, Mrs. Roosevelt indicated that she had not been persuaded; she merely noted that a woman had been to see her, "urging a most interesting peace plan," involving "the abandonment of all armaments which could possibly be used anywhere except along our shores." Jeannette continued for some time to believe in Mrs. Roosevelt's desire for peace, and for several years urged the staff of the National Council for the Prevention of War to be sure to send the Council's Christmas message to the White House.

That summer, after the exertions of the preceding months and years, she was desperately in need of a holiday, and on July 28 she took off for Europe, accompanied by her nephew John R. Kinney, who planned to study in Heidelberg. She wrote to a friend later that her stay in Germany was too short to make her sensitive to the warlike drives beneath the orderly landscape. After six weeks in the Scandinavian countries, France and England, she missed a return trip on the *Queen Mary*, but took passage to Canada on the *Duchess of Richmond* (of which she wrote to Libby that it was familiarly known as *The Drunken Duchess*), arriving back in Washington on September 10.

She had barely time enough to settle into her home in Watkinsville and collect her thoughts when an alarm of particularly sinister implications, to her mind, sounded throughout the land, and indeed throughout the world, showing how far the administration was prepared to go toward military confrontation. In October the President gave his famous "quarantine" speech in Chicago in which he maintained that all civilization stood in danger of destruction from the ruthless actions of certain (unnamed) powers, and that "there must be a concerted effort of the peace-loving nations to restrain the marauders. . . ." It was difficult to reconcile these noble sentiments with the fact that American oil and scrap iron were flowing to Japan and China and that German and Italian aircraft continued to rain bombs at will over Spain.

To Jeannette and her associates Roosevelt's declaration meant that he had abandoned the pretense of neutrality and was determined to get us into war. Once more she took to the lecture platform, giving 149 speeches to audiences of almost 34,000, as well as fourteen radio talks between October 1937 and June of the following year. One of her most telling comments during this lecture tour was in answer to the charge that she was indifferent to the suffering of nations attacked without cause. "Do I want to help China?" she asked. "Of course I want to help China, but I am not going to throw myself out of a seventeenth-story window to help China. It wouldn't help China." Again and again she repeated her central theme: There would always be disputes between nations, but none of them was ever settled by wars. If culprits had to be found for starting wars, she held, the guiltier parties were the richer, larger, stronger countries rather than the "have-nots."

But to many people in America the "have-nots" had no more justification for seeking military solutions to their problems than the "haves" had had in imposing intolerable conditions on their enemies. Wars are begotten by other wars, going back to the dawn of history, with one injustice replacing another, with hope rising eternally that the next war will settle matters forever. Jeannette saw that all her fervor and all her eloquence were unavailing; the country was moving inexoraby toward the involvement she feared so much. In 1939, only five years after the Vinson-Trammel Act, the President called for the appropriation of more than a billion dollars to expand the navy still further. Leaders of industry who had formerly found Roosevelt's expenditures for relief communistic now commended him as a far-sighted statesman; newspapers that had for years been critical of his policies now heaped praise on him; business began to pick up after the recession of 1937. And as the world situation came to a crisis in Munich in September 1938, former advocates of peace fell away in great numbers to join in the cry for action against the Fascist powers in both hemispheres.

Jeannette now began to ask herself whether there was yet time to put a finger in the dike. Her lobbying efforts, once so effectual, were frustrated; her speaking tours reached only a small fraction of the population; her sponsoring organization, the National Council for the Prevention of War, was more impecunious than ever and was losing its adherents. Living as she did on very short rations, she had pleaded with Libby to let her work for six months in the year at $300 a month, which would permit her to pay her bills in Georgia and seek gainful employment elsewhere for the rest of the year, or perhaps stay with her family in Montana at little or no expense. But Libby insisted on a monthly stipend of $150 for twelve months, and as we have seen even this small sum came in irregularly. By 1938 it had stopped altogether. "I've no doubt money is slow coming in," she wrote to him at this time, "but if you can send me some or put me on a weekly payroll it will help a lot. It hurts my spirit so to be broke."

Libby was no more liberal with others on his staff than he was with Jeannette; he assumed that all of them were so wrapped up in the peace movement that they would be willing to work for nothing if necessary in order to take part in the great crusade. Moreover, he was aware of the fact that Jeannette had a wealthy brother who was devoted to her and who could be relied upon to provide her with the necessities of life. Her sister Edna believed that her "poverty" was purely voluntary, writing that

> she had a peculiar sort of neurosis of wanting to appear poor. . . . She seemed to enjoy living in privation as though it were indecent to have any money. Wellington would give her ample money if she were to go on a trip. She would live penuriously and save money and as soon as she returned home she would give Wellington whatever money she had not spent.

Jeannette's attitude toward money had perhaps another basis, stemming from her feminist belief that every woman should be self-supporting; she also took pride in being able to adjust her standard of living to the scale of what she herself could earn, however little that might be. (Certain penny-pinching habits remained with her all her life, even when they were no longer necessary, but it was characteristic of her that these related principally to her own comfort, not to the comfort of her friends.) Libby showed himself somewhat insensitive in not realizing her need to be paid for work done, as a laborer worthy of her hire.

There were temperamental differences between these two pacifists also, irreconcilable differences. Jeannette's career had been built on immediate contact with the people, or more particularly with voters, whom she approached always with concrete plans for action. Libby on the other hand was more comfortable in the company of persons of power and wealth who might be won over to support his views. "I loved raising money," he confessed, but his success in this endeavor was limited by the unpleasant fact that most rich people had a fatal tendency to invest in more profitable enterprises. Jeannette resented him on other grounds: she thought that because she was a woman he did not take her advice often enough, but preferred to follow the counsels of men with far less political experience than she had had. The deteriorating world situation hastened the break. In May 1938 she asked for a six months' leave of absence, and the following March she resigned from the National Council.

During the thirties Jeannette gave herself with passion to two aspects of the peace movement: first, seeking ways leading to the abolition of war everywhere in the world, as in her support of the Kellogg-Briand Pact, the London Naval Conference, the World Court and the Geneva Disarmament Conference; then, concentrating on keeping the United States out of foreign wars, as in her support of the Ludlow amendment and the Neutrality Acts, and by extension her resistance to the expansion of the navy to a point where it could be used for aggressive purposes. She was not then in favor of unilateral disarmament, as she was to be later in her career, but approved of effective measures for the military defense of the country, "preparedness" for possible attack. As early as 1934 she had said in a speech that air power made the navy useless except for transporting and conveying troops overseas, not foreseeing perhaps how deadly an engine of war the airplane could become. She also was an early proponent of the plan to combine air, ground and naval forces in one Department of Defense to bring about greater efficiency, stressing, however, that the united military branch should be limited to defense. In this she was seconded by men of far less pacifistic views who saw in a single Department of Defense a far more useful vehicle for expanding our military forces than the three independent services acting independently and often in competition with one another.

And further to support her argument that the country needed no more than adequate defenses to keep out of wars, she declared in a speech at the University of Virginia in 1937 that the United States could not be attacked successfully, thanks to the barriers of two mighty oceans. In a speech in Helena in the late thirties she explained that she did not want the United States to be so defenseless as to *invite* a foreign invasion. Calling for a "highly modernized, mechanized military defense . . . in peace-

Testifying before the House Naval Affairs Committee in February 1939 in opposition to further naval expansion.

United Press International Photo

time—so perfected that . . . no enemy can reach us," she maintained that "When an enemy . . . is aware that our shores are impregnable . . . they [*sic*] will not waste time crossing the ocean." Then, in an analogy to which later events lent a certain irony, she declared that she wanted our coasts to be "as impregnable as Corregidor." This view did not take into account the fact that because of earlier territorial expansion our possessions now included two distant, vulnerable island outposts, Hawaii and the Philippines.

Granted that these were mistakes in judgment, they were no more faulty than those of men in positions of power who, despite a huge expansion of our naval and air forces by 1941, were unable to prevent the disaster at Pearl Harbor. Nor was she so far out of the mainstream of American beliefs as might be supposed. She herself was certain that there was a strong body of opinion in the country that reasoned as she did, and that she was needed to give it a voice in Washington. She wanted a constituency, a mass of voters who would authorize her to act in their behalf in Congress. Such a constituency was not to be had in Georgia; Vinson had made that clear.

She decided to return to Montana.

IX

Replay in Congress

Jeannette had always retained her voting residence in Montana, but twenty years had elapsed since she had served as its representative in Congress. If she was to run again she would be obliged to make herself known once more to the people there, and particularly to young people who might never have heard of her. In 1939 she was fifty-nine, old enough to be a grandmother; notwithstanding her acknowledged place in Montana's history, she was in fact a newcomer to a whole generation of voters. Moreover, she would need financial support for her campaign. On arriving in Montana therefore she consulted first with Wellington, who agreed that she had a very good chance to win. "Of course I wouldn't have run if Wellington hadn't approved," she said later, "because he would have to pay for it."

Once assured of Wellington's moral and financial backing, she began her campaign for the nomination a year ahead of time in a totally unorthodox fashion: She addressed herself to the children as a means of publicizing her candidacy to their parents. Since the state was now divided into two congressional districts, it was not necessary for her to cover the entire state, as in her first campaign, but she intended to leave no corner of her area untouched.* After studying the geographical disposition of every

* Thanks to a decision of the U.S. Supreme Court, the First District, which she sought to represent, now contained a more equitable distribution of Republicans and Democrats than in 1918.

Campaign photograph used when Miss Rankin ran for Congress in 1940.

high school in her district, she drew up an itinerary and sent a letter to each school principal telling him when she would be available to speak at the school assembly. With great cunning she attached no return address to these communications in order not to risk a refusal. Over a period of two months, five days a week, she gave talks at fifty-two of the fifty-six high schools in the district.

Her formula was everywhere the same; to establish herself as a native of Montana, like them; to tell them about the threat of war and what they could do about it, how they could take part in the democratic process.

She directed her appeal particularly to the girls. When she was a child, she said, a visiting congressman speaking before the school assembly would address most of his remarks to the boys. Then he would turn to the girls and say: "Perhaps one day you'll be the wife of a President of the United States." But since that time women had won the vote and other rights, Jeannette added, and someday we'd have a woman President. Hoots from the boys would greet this. She would continue: "There are opportunities for girls now, and opportunities for boys too. Someday one of you may be the husband of a President." The boys were more subdued on hearing this ominous prediction.

Then she would go on to the real message of her talk, which was to win them over to the struggle for peace. And she told them the story of her classmate whose mother had handed him as a baby to the Indian chief as a peace offering, thereby preventing a massacre of the settlers with whom she was crossing the plains. In conclusion she explained how they could help prevent another war: "Talk to your parents about this; tell them to write to the President that they don't want this country to go to war again." She also urged them to do something on their own: "You can't hand the President a baby, but you too can write him a letter. You don't have to say that you're high school students. You mustn't lie, but when you write to him, don't tell him how old you are. *I* never do." And she closed amid roars of laughter. From many persons known and unknown to her she received ample evidence that the students did speak to their parents about her lively talks at their schools. As a public relations scheme it was not only clever, but inexpensive as well.

She did no campaigning beyond this before the primaries. Filing for the Republican nomination for Congress in June 1940, she won against a field of three men. After an absence of twenty years from the Montana political scene she had surfaced again and had quickly become a factor to reckon with. Her election campaign was conducted in as unorthodox a fashion as her primary campaign, although now she addressed herself to adults rather than to children. A handbill issued from her headquarters listed her supporters as distinguished persons from all over the country: Ruth Hanna McCormick Simms, former representative in Congress; Senators McNary (Oregon), Champ Clark (Missouri), Taft (Ohio), Robert LaFollette, Jr. (Wisconsin), Tobey and Bridges (New Hampshire), and Frazier (North Dakota); Representatives Knutsen (Minnesota), Tinkham (Massachusetts), Brewster (Maine), and Woodruff (Michigan); Mayor LaGuardia of New York; President Green of the American Federation of Labor; Bruce Barton, the nation's number one press agent; and Katharine Anthony, author! Not a single sponsor from Montana. Presumably she had headquarters, or an office, but her address at this time was Avalanche Ranch, Wellington's home. She chose to drive all over the district alone, without a chauffeur, stopping on her way to meetings to ask men on the streets of a town or at work in the fields their views about war or the preparation for war. As of old, she approached women in shops or in their kitchens to talk things over. It was not her way to foist a handshake on total strangers, but rather to attempt a dialogue. Making her appeal particularly to women and to working people, she relied on the antiwar sentiment in the state to win. In a radio speech she denied that she opposed an adequate system of defense for the country; on the contrary she would have the existing arrangements perfected. It was not an external foe from whom we had most to fear, she said; the real enemies of the nation were hunger, want, unemployment and disease.

Her Democratic opponent was the incumbent, Jerry O'Connell, who had gained a reputation as a New Dealer with a liberal record and who did not differ with her greatly on the war issue. She had no compunction about contesting his seat, however, for she felt she was more firmly dedicated to a peace program than he was, or indeed than any other possible rival. The copper interests no longer dominated Montana politics as they had in her earlier campaigns, but along with other giant corporations they still exercised considerable power in the state. Still, in this particular election they were helpless, as Jeannette put it in later years. "They couldn't work for Jerry . . . or I'd get elected. They couldn't work for me, or Jerry would be elected. So they kept their hands off, and we really had an expression of public opinion, because the Company couldn't get involved." The Republican party machine of course gave her no assistance. When her sister Grace went into Republican headquarters in Missoula on election day to ask how the vote was going for Jeannette Rankin, she was told: "Oh, she'll never make it; she comes from Georgia."

She did make it, winning with a plurality of 9,264 votes.

Her arrival in Washington as Congressman from Montana in January 1941 was not attended by the celebrations and tributes that had marked her first election. A small number of women had followed her to the Capitol since her maiden appearance, and although none had exceeded her in energy and intelligence, the novelty had worn off. The spittoons had vanished from the floor of the House, and there was a well-appointed ladies' room easily accessible to women members and their secretaries. Jeannette's secretaries, Sigrid Scannell and Rosanell Maitland, were under far less pressure than were her aides in 1917; the volume of mail was not so great, and Jeannette's appointments to the Insular Affairs and the Public Lands Committees offered her little chance to take a stand on the all-important question. A visitor to her office reported the presence of a caged canary—an oddity in those quarters—but in truth the bird belonged to Jeannette's mother. Jeannette herself preferred dogs.

The atmosphere in Washington in 1941 might well have given her a sense of *déjà vu;* as in 1917, the Great Powers were at war all over the world while the United States was still at peace; supplies and aid of all kinds were flowing from America to England in support of the Atlantic Community; propaganda machines were working full blast in favor of both sides in the conflict; and the war-based economy had begun to eliminate the specter of unemployment as mills, mines and farms found outlets for their goods in provisioning the embattled nations. Sentiment in the country was sharply divided between those who greatly feared the cruelty, persecutions and passion for conquest shown by the Axis powers, and those few who either admired the German dictator or were willing to come to terms with him as representing "the wave of the future." Among the latter were members of the America First Committee, made up of those whose tolerance of or sympathy with the Nazis went hand in hand with their loathing of Franklin Roosevelt and the whole New Deal program. In spite of their opposition to our entrance into the war, Jeannette shrank from joining the America Firsters, for in their ranks were reactionaries whose economic and social views ran counter to her own. Perhaps she knew intuitively that these men were not so much against war in general as against this particular war. There were in fact few who shared Jeannette's simple belief that any war was immoral and settled nothing.

Her sense of foreboding that war was imminent was intensified when Eleanor Roosevelt invited her to a conference of prominent women at the White House. Those present included

Frances Perkins, Mrs. Felix Frankfurter, Senator Margaret Chase Smith, and the few other women then serving as members of Congress. It was stressed that the meeting was confidential. Jeannette, who had long believed that the President's wife was deeply committed to the cause of peace, became alarmed when the purpose of the conference was disclosed: Mrs. Roosevelt wanted a group of women well known throughout the country to come to the support of the President if an emergency should arise. Frances Perkins must have realized that Jeannette was far from ready to consent to such a blanket proposal, for as they walked out of the room she tried to win her compliance by saying that their old friend Florence Kelley would have favored it. Jeannette was disturbed by the hush-hush aspect of the affair and became even more uneasy when three weeks later, while she was alone in her office late in the day, she received a telephone call from Mrs. Roosevelt's secretary that there was no more need for secrecy about the conference. She suspected, perhaps without reason, that a trap had been laid for her, that she would later be charged with having been willing to support the President under any circumstances, even a declaration of war. But she did not trust even those who believed in war only as a last resort.

Like many crusaders, Jeannette had a healthy ego. She knew that she was right; moreover, she was convinced that there were millions of voiceless people all over the country for whom she was the only spokesman. After all, had she not been elected on an antiwar platform by the voters of Montana? She would not be silent; she would not accept the inevitability of war. A few weeks after she took office she seized the first opportunity that presented itself to check the trend toward American involvement. On February 8 she rose to offer an amendment to the gigantic defense bill, proposing that special congressional approval be required before any of our armed forces could be sent abroad. Her amendment was defeated by a vote of 137 to 82, showing that she was not totally without supporters.

On May 6, apropos of Mothers' Day, she offered a resolution to the same effect: "Congress hereby declares that it is the policy of the United States not to send the armed forces of the United States to fight in any place outside the Western Hemisphere or insular possessions of the United States." In presenting this resolution she claimed to speak for the women of America, who agreed on the necessity of protecting our shores from foreign invaders but did not want to have their sons "sacrificed for the profits of a few or because some wish to decide the problems of Europe by the war method." Foiled in this attempt, she took another tack in remembrance of the role played by Allied propagandists in World War I: she asked to have printed in the *Congressional Record* a statement issued by some 500 New York women demanding that English-born Americans like Bishop Manning and Frank Kingdon refrain from calling for our intervention in the war. Again on June 6 she offered another amendment to the defense bill, providing that no appropriation in the measure for the pay of our armed forces be used to send the army or air force to fight in foreign lands outside the Americas and our insular possessions. This too was defeated, 73 to 39.

The current was running against her, but she would not yield; she would not admit that it was too late. When Congress reconvened after the summer recess she tried once more to stem the tide in the debate on repeal of Section 6 of the 1939 Neutrality Act. This provided that American merchant vessels should not be armed in time of war between other nations. Mindful of how instrumental the arming of American ships had been in drawing us into World War I, she pleaded for the retention of Section 6:

> Does not the gentleman consider it an invitation for the destruction of our seamen to announce that our merchant vessels are armed, to announce to the American people that they are armed sufficiently to protect themselves, and then to send out ships that are insufficiently armed and manned by men untrained and incapable of protecting the ship?

This would be in effect an invitation to belligerents to fire on any American merchant ship, whatever its ability to withstand attack, she maintained, because there was no way of knowing whether it was armed or not. The bill repealing Section 6 came to a vote on November 13 and was passed 212 to 194, with 22 not voting, a better showing than the anti-administration forces had made up to then, but little cause for rejoicing on Jeannette's part.

She would not desist. On October 30 she introduced a bill

requiring that propaganda disseminated by agents of foreign powers be designated as such. This never reached the calendar. Nor did her next attempt, a resolution presented on November 28 calling for a national advisory election to ascertain the will of the people before war could be declared. Frustrated in all her attempts to keep the country from going over the brink, she sought crumbs of comfort where she could. Like General George C. Marshall, she anticipated the swift collapse of Russia under the Nazi onslaught, and she found this a desirable eventuality in that it might lead to a better understanding between the United States and Japan!

The nation was headed toward war, although no one foresaw the act that would catapult us into it, Jeannette no more than anyone else, for much of her thinking at that time was shaped by the Nye Committee revelations concerning Allied propagandists, munitions makers, and the arming of merchant vessels. She had long affirmed her support of measures to make our coasts and insular possessions impregnable to attack. Could not the country rely on our armed forces, to which so much treasure had been entrusted, she asked, to repel an attack from any quarter?

On December 7, 1941, Jeannette entrained at Washington to go to Detroit, where she was to give a speech the next day on her usual theme: how to keep the country out of war. Settling into her upper berth for the night, she turned on her radio and heard the news of the Japanese attack on Pearl Harbor. A war resolution was being prepared, she learned, and Roosevelt would address the people. Like millions of others, she did not sleep that night; she dressed quickly and got off the train at Pittsburgh to wait for the next train back to Washington. There she got into her car and drove around all morning, alone, to make sure that nobody could reach her. Seeing the streets of the capital already thronged with soldiers, she got "madder and madder," as she told a friend later.

This time she would not consult anyone, not even Wellington; she was not going to suffer the anguish of doubt she had known in April 1917, or put others through the strain of trying to persuade her to do what she felt was wrong. Nothing then known or since divulged could change her belief that Roosevelt's policies had forced the Japanese to take this irrevocable step, even though it was carried out with deception and treachery, while the Japanese ambassadors were still in Washington conferring with members of the administration. War was evil; it settled nothing, and she would not be a party to it, whatever the consequences to her and to her career.

And indeed this time she would have to stand quite alone in both houses of Congress. There was no Robert LaFollette to give an air of some authority to the antiwar position in the Senate now; there was no Claude Kitchin in the House to declare that it took no courage to declare a war for others to fight. The attack on Pearl Harbor united the country as it had not been united in the Wilson era, for the people were aware only of the "unprovoked" attack, not of the maneuvering and secret arrangements that had preceded it. Most of those who had applauded Jeannette's peace activities earlier were now relieved that at last the United States would take up arms against the forces of evil as represented by the Axis powers; she would not have their sympathy or their moral support. Even before the war resolution came to a vote she sensed how truly alone she would be.

In the course of her drive around Washington on the morning of December 8, Jeannette resolved that this time, unlike on that earlier occasion, she would speak to her fellow congressmen and explain her position, make one last plea to stop the mass killing that was to come. As soon as the joint resolution declaring war on Japan was read in the House, therefore, she rose and cried: "Mr. Speaker, I object!" Speaker Rayburn cut her short: "You're out of order!" Since, save for Miss Rankin, the House seemed to be unanimous, not much time was needed for the debate, which lasted only forty minutes. Again and again she rose to address the chair: "Mr. Speaker, I would like to be heard!" "Mr. Speaker, a point of order!" Rayburn would not recognize her, and there were shouts from the benches: "Sit down, sister!" What she was trying to do was to have the resolution referred to committee, which would delay the fateful decision and allow her time to speak at some length on the reasons for not going to war. But in that highly charged atmosphere the members were too impatient to follow normal parliamentary procedure; war was men's business, and no silly woman could be allowed to get in the way.

Several congressmen came to sit beside her and urge her to vote with them, arguing that there was no question about the attack. "They really did bomb Pearl Harbor," said one member. "That makes no difference," she answered; "killing more people won't help matters." Everett Dirksen, then a congressman from Illinois and even at that time a power in the Republican party, approached her with more compassion than the others. "Does it have to be?" he asked. "Yes," was her reply. "Well," the gravelly voice said, "we'll stand by you." Whether he meant by this that the party would stand by her, or that the gallant representatives would protect her from patrioteers who might have torn her limb from limb is not clear.

At the first roll call her "nay" was spoken in a firm, clear voice. "As a woman I can't go to war, and I refuse to send anyone else," she added, again violating protocol. The vote was 388 to 1. But whereas in 1917 her negative vote had been received with some sympathy, as representing the tender conscience of a gentle woman, now she was met with active hostility. According to an Associated Press report, "a chorus of hisses and boos" arose from the floor and the galleries when her vote was heard. And when she went out into the cloakroom after the roll call a group of young army officers advanced toward her and reviled her for her stand. She did not flinch under this assault but drew closer to them, sniffed their breath, and said sternly, "You've been drinking!" Nor did she meet any friendly faces as she left the Capitol. In fact the crowd at the door seemed so hostile that the Capitol police feared she might be assaulted. She took refuge in a phone booth and then made her way to her office, locking herself in.

Press reaction to her vote was almost universally condemnatory, and it was left to only one old case-hardened newspaper editor to give her her due:

> Probably 100 men in Congress would have liked to do what she did [wrote William Allen White in the *Emporia Gazette* on December 10]. Not one of them had the courage to do it. The *Gazette* entirely disagrees with the wisdom of her position. But Lord, it was a brave thing! . . . When in one hundred years from now, courage, sheer courage based on moral indignation, is celebrated in this country, the name of Jeannette Rankin,

After voting "No" on the declaration of war against Japan in December 1941, Miss Rankin was obliged to take refuge in a phone booth to escape hostile demonstrators.

United Press International Photo

> who stood firm in folly for her faith, will be written in monumental bronze not for what she did but for the way she did it.*

But White's view was exceptional. A member of the Montana Republican National Committee pleaded with her to change her vote in order to redeem Montana's honor. Jeannette might have reflected that Montana's honor was indeed a delicate plant if it could be nourished only by the shedding of vast quantities of blood.

Among the letters she received commending her on her vote was one from Emily Greene Balch, who had been a peace activist ever since World War I and who was to win the Nobel Peace Prize in 1946; but Mrs. Balch, while granting that Jeannette had shown courage in sticking to what she thought was right, confessed that she herself had changed her mind in this particular case.

The Nobel Peace Prize was never conferred on Jeannette, perhaps for the reason that she believed wars must be stopped

* Fortunately she did not have to wait a century for rehabilitation in the eyes of the public. Only seventeen years later John F. Kennedy published his "Three Women of Courage" in *McCall's Magazine* in which he ranked her as among the most fearless characters in American history.

before, not after, they had begun. She explained this to Libby when she told him that in her vote against the war declaration she had been guided by her whole philosophy of life, for without such a set of beliefs "others make the decisions for you in a time of crisis." And she repeated an old adage of the suffrage movement: "You can trust the woman who believed in suffrage, but you can never trust the woman who just wanted to vote."

What she called her philosophy of life would have to sustain her for the rest of her term in Congress, for the big war machine went into high gear immediately, and its roar drowned out the small voice of the Congressman from Montana. When the resolutions declaring war on Germany and Italy came before the House she voted "present" but made no effort to speak. For the rest she participated in but few debates, limiting herself mainly to the discussion of draft exemptions or deferments and other means of mitigating the effects of the war on various special groups. On December 15, 1941, however, she rose to object to the imposition of the death penalty for willful sabotage against national defense, but she was not sustained. War itself inflicted the death penalty on so many it was absurd to expect Congress to show mercy toward a few saboteurs. In March 1942 she spoke in favor of direct relief for Indians whose menfolk had been drafted or were obliged to go far from their homes to obtain jobs in war industry, leaving a great many women without means of subsistence. "These are the most needy people in the whole country," she argued. In June 1942 she introduced a bill designed to give the government a longer period in which to uncover and prosecute fraudulent operators and contractors of war goods than the statute of limitations would permit. This proposal grew out of testimony before the Nye Committee which revealed that some patently crooked suppliers in World War I had escaped Federal prosecution because their shady deals had not come to light until after the statutory limit.

The members of the House, however, were not moved by the plight of the Indians, nor did they see eye to eye with Jeannette on draft deferments or unprincipled war contractors. They would probably have been even less interested in a bill she was trying to draw up on the money question. It will be remembered that in the thirties she had advanced an elaborate scheme for a system of fiat money to be used in wartime, a scheme which presumably would eliminate the possibility of swollen war profits for either capital or labor. Although in her presentation of that plan before the House Military Affairs Committee she had seemed more ironic than serious, the money question had engaged her interest for many years. The bill she was working on now may have had some useful concepts, or it may have been another one of those "cracked-brained" money schemes that have so often come out of the West, but what its terms were is not known, for it never took precise form, and Jeannette was reluctant to talk about it. Nevertheless, it shows how wide was the range of her concerns and how fertile her mind in seeking solutions to the problems that beset American society.

As her second term in Congress drew to a close, she found it intolerable, high-spirited as she was, to let it terminate without once having had the opportunity to explain herself and define her position. With all the war bills that were being rushed through the House, she knew she would be granted no time in which to do this on the floor, so she chose to have her remarks printed in the *Congressional Record*, where they stand as a vindication of her intransigence in opposing the war, but even more strikingly as an indictment of the Roosevelt administration for double-dealing.

The date was December 8, 1942, and she opened by saying that she was taking advantage of the anniversary of Pearl Harbor to raise "pertinent questions, not out of any spirit of disunity, but in a firm belief that the Nation's welfare requires a vigilant exercise of the traditional American right of free inquiry." Pearl Harbor she described as a thunderbolt, the greatest in American history. Could the attack have been foreseen? Yes, she said, for there was general knowledge that American military power would be needed to prevent the dissolution of the British and Dutch empires in the Far East. And she quoted the *Christian Century* of November 19, 1941, in which it was stated that "the whole structure of the white empires is threatening to fall apart unless we intervene in Asia." According to this article, the British would welcome American involvement in Japan. She then went on to quote from the book of an Englishman named Rogerson who as early as 1938 had anticipated what role the United

States could be induced to play in the preservation of the British Empire. In this book, *Propaganda in the Next War* (probably designed for study by the staff of the British Foreign Office), Rogerson had written that it would be much more difficult to persuade the United States to take Britain's part in the next world war than it had been in 1917. "It will need a definite threat to America. . . . The position will naturally be considerably eased if Japan were involved and this might bring America in without further ado. . . . *It would be a natural and obvious object of our propagandists to achieve this* [italics added]."

Thus if America were to be brought into the war, Jeannette continued, an overt act of aggression by Japan would be necessary. Churchill was so aware of this that when he met Roosevelt in the waters off Newfoundland for the Atlantic Conference in August 1941 he asked the President to join him in delivering an ultimatum to Japan. As her source for this she cited an article in the *Ladies' Home Journal* for July 1942 by Forrest Davis and Ernest K. Lindley, the latter a close friend of Roosevelt's. Henry Luce had repeated the allegation in *Life* magazine for July 20, 1942, stating that Roosevelt had issued the ultimatum to Japan that led to the Pearl Harbor attack, although in Luce's view this had been done to help China.

In his message to Congress describing the negotiations with Japan prior to December 7, the President had not admitted the dispatch of an ultimatum, but he did go so far as to say that he had asked Japan to accept the principle of "nondisturbance of the status quo in the Pacific." This was equivalent to asking Japan to guarantee the white men's empires in the Orient, Jeannette pointed out, and committed "American lives, fortunes and prestige to securing a guarantee for British and Dutch imperial interests."

Within a week of the agreement between the President and Churchill at the Atlantic Conference, economic sanctions were invoked, and by October 24 raw material shortages in Japan were acute. "Was it not strange," Jeannette asked, that Mr. Roosevelt, who for years had refused "to enforce the Neutrality Act of 1936 to prevent shipment of war materials to Japan," and had therefore "largely contributed to supplying that nation with the raw materials for the armament now being used against our own troops"—was it not strange that he should suddenly have "changed his policy and cut off not only war supplies but virtually everything required by the civilian population as well?"

As a result of the agreement at the Atlantic Conference, she maintained, an *incident* was required. Pearl Harbor, therefore, in reality came as no surprise to the President. During the weeks preceding the attack frequent warnings of the possibility had been sent to the commanders in the Pacific, and our forces had been put on the alert. She quoted a U.S. Navy officer on duty in the Pacific in November of 1941, Lieutenant Clarence E. Dickinson, who told that his orders were to protect the secrecy of his mission and if need be to shoot "anything we saw in the sky and to bomb anything we saw on the sea." On the president's orders, the navy was not to wait for a formal declaration of war. Having provoked an incident, therefore, the President and his advisers ought not to profess to have been surprised by the attack itself; they could only have been shocked by its overwhelming success.

Churchill was not slow, she continued, to claim credit for obtaining Roosevelt's complicity. American participation in the war was what he had "dreamed of, aimed at, and worked for," he said in a speech before the House of Commons soon after Pearl Harbor. In her one humorous aside in the course of this sober recital Jeannette quoted Congressman Hatton W. Summers of Texas, who admitted: "This blaming the Pearl Harbor tragedy on the treachery of the Japs is like the fellow who had been tickling the hind leg of a mule trying to explain his bunged-up condition by blaming the mule for having abused his confidence."

Jeannette ended with a defense of the traditional American rights of free speech and free inquiry, implying that she would continue to ask and seek answers to all the questions she had raised. Her concluding paragraph was bitter:

> A year ago, one of my congressional colleagues, having observed for months the adroitness with which President Roosevelt had brought us ever closer to the brink of war in the Atlantic only to be continually frustrated in the final step by a reluctant Congress, seeing fate present the President on December 7, 1941, with a *casus belli* beyond all criticism—exclaimed in despair: "What luck that man has!"

At the time Jeannette wrote this bill of particulars she was one of the very few in this country who saw the sequence of events leading up to our participation in World War II so clearly; scholarly research since then, based on access to secret documents, has reinforced her charges. Her basic thesis, moreover, that the people of the United States are, on the whole, peace-loving, and that they can be led into a war only by the practice of the most disingenuous deceit and mystification by their leaders, has been painfully illustrated once more in recent times by the disclosure of events leading up to the war in Vietnam.

Jeannette's December 8 (printed) speech fell like a stone in roiling waters, leaving no ripples, unremarked, unheard. In 1917 she had felt the reverberations of her vote against the war for a long time, cheers and howls emanating from admirers and detractors. Now there was no outcry; she was "just ignored," she told an interviewer long afterward. The country was prosecuting the greatest war in its history, committing all its resources, human and material, to engagements all over the globe; statesmen were pronouncing sentiments of high moral purpose to which many who had opposed our entrance into the war subscribed; unemployment was a thing of the past, so there were no mutterings from the bottom of the heap. Jeannette was completely out of step with the times, and she knew it. She once said to a friend that she never worried about anything she couldn't do anything about. Still there was the horror of it, the certainty that though the war might end in victory for "our side," it would not end in peace. Added to this was the frustration of knowing that all her work for a quarter of a century had gone for naught. Her congressional career, too, was at an end, with nothing achieved save that lonely protest. Still it was a protest that she hoped would give her stature as time went on and leave her at ease with her own conscience.

X

Going Around the World

Serving in Congress is not the road to wealth, or even to a competence, unless one establishes cozy relationships with certain vested interests that can offer a well-paying job or an opportunity to make profitable investments after retiring from office. In such arrangements there is always a quid pro quo, not necessarily corrupt but at the very least showing a benign concern for local business or industrial potentates. Jeannette had never established such relationships; moreover, the "interests" she represented were always penniless and were more likely to ask her for a contribution than to give her one. The timing of her two terms in Congress also made it difficult for her to put anything by, however modest her scale of living, for the emoluments of a congressman during her first term were $7,500 a year; they were later raised to $10,000, which was what she earned in her second term, but a few years later they were raised again to $15,000 with perquisites for staff and secretarial work that she had never enjoyed.

Her meager income might have been one of the factors that led her to return to Montana to live in 1943, but there was also some pressure from her brother and sisters to bring her back to the bosom of her family. In this they were no doubt sensitive to the pain and frustration she was suffering with regard to the war, but they also appealed to her filial feelings as well. In 1943 her mother was over ninety and, although still alert, was infirm enough to need constant care. Jeannette's relations with her mother had always been very close, ties based on mutual reliance and respect dating back to her girlhood. In Jeannette's first term in Congress Mrs. Rankin had helped to run the Washington household, and on every possible occasion thereafter she had visited with her daughter in Georgia, visits returned by Jeannette on her holidays in Montana. Jeannette accepted the fact of her mother's declining health when Mrs. Rankin could no longer take the long trip to Georgia to be with her.

For the next few years Jeannette's main occupation was to look after her mother's comfort, the role so often assigned to maiden ladies of limited means. It was mortifying for her to leave the bustle and excitement of what had become the world's capital, a city where she had held some rank and a degree of power, however limited, and return home as a sort of superior nurse. Mrs. Rankin spent her summers at Wellington's ranch, where Jeannette and Edna looked after her; her winters were passed at Coeur d'Alene, Idaho, with her daughter Grace Kinney. There were compensations in this arrangement for Jeannette in that she saw more of her relatives and their attractive families than had been possible for many years. Wellington had become the wealthiest man in the state of Montana through his land holdings and was now a dominant figure in the state's Republican Party. Like all the Rankins he was extremely hospitable, and at his ranch Jeannette could generally find interesting company.

After twenty-five years as a successful lawyer Wellington had gained a fortune in the thirties, when one huge ranch after another went into bankruptcy or was taken over by the banks to which they were mortgaged. It became a common practice for the local bankers to offer him a property when it was relinquished by its owners, and Wellington was astute enough to turn it into a paying proposition. Sometimes he made a quick profit by breaking up a huge ranch with a large overhead into several smaller operations; in other cases he was successful merely because of superior management. This was due in large part to his knowledge of how to hire and hold on to his help, for one of the most difficult problems in running a ranch is to assemble a dependable labor force. The romantic cowhand of legend and the movies was in reality a hard-drinking, scrappy fellow, nomadic in temperament, ignorant of everything save the handling of horses and cattle. Wellington had known the breed since his boyhood.

Jeannette enjoyed seeing her brother function in his professional and business affairs, probably the more so as they shared many of the same traits: a capacity for management, an interest in people, a sense of humor, and an overriding passion for politics. For all his worldly success Wellington still yearned for elective office, and particuarly for a seat in the United States Senate, where his old friend and boon companion, Burton K. Wheeler, had held forth for so many years. In 1944 he decided to chance it again and run for the other Senate seat, in the belief that after twelve years of Democratic rule the country was ready to switch over to the Republicans. His commanding position in the Montana Republican Party assured him of winning the nomination, and with Jeannette's help he felt confident this time that he would make it. It was a welcome distraction for Jeannette, who threw herself into the campaign with ardor. But with the war still raging, the voters seemed reluctant to throw the Democratic rascals out, and once again Wellington had to accept defeat.

There is a certain pathos in his misjudgment of the situation in his own case, while when Jeannette chose to run for office he was generally correct. Jeannette was in fact better attuned to the moods of the electorate than her brother; she was closer to the concerns of simple people, concerns which Wellington, a man of wealth, had less occasion to know in any but the most superficial sense. He continued to nourish hopes for elective office, however, almost to the end of his life. Fourteen years later, when Jeannette was in India, he called her on the telephone from Montana and spoke to her at some length. Although he did not mention any current political ambitions during their talk, on reflection she came to the conclusion that he wanted her to encourage him in another bid for the Senate seat. But he did not bring up the subject, and she did not in all conscience think it was worth the effort.

The care of her mother was not so time-consuming as to

abridge Jeannette's abiding interest in national and world events. While the war went on she remained on the sidelines and kept her own counsel. Her mind was not idle, however; it was churning with plans for the future. Deprived of an active role in affairs, she had time for introspection, time to review her past campaigns and refine her theories about how to stop nations from going to war. The ongoing war was one of those things she could do nothing about, and there was no point in beating out her brains in vain regrets. As a loyal American and with young friends and relatives engaged in the fighting on many fronts, moreover, she could not wish for her country to be defeated for the sole purpose of teaching warmongers a lesson. On the other hand, she was almost prostrated with grief and guilt when the atomic bombs were dropped on Hiroshima and Nagasaki. That it should have been Harry Truman who pressed the button to rain death and destruction on those two cities far from the war front came as no surprise to her. Back in the thirties, when Truman was first elected to the Senate, she had approached him about some legislative matter and had spoken of her horror of war. "Well," said Truman, "I've always liked war. I feel we made all our advances in civilization from war."

When the war was at last over she was ready to start out on a new project. The peace movement had collapsed, and she sensed no groundswell that promised even a slim chance of a comeback in politics for a person of her opinions. But politics was only one of her passions; travel was another. Whenever she found no role in the political arena she took to the road, to see how people lived in other countries, to learn their hopes and fears, pursuing her education through the most intense observation of which she was capable. The world was her university. As a young woman she had visited New Zealand to see for herself the workings of a country where women could vote. She had been to Europe three times and in the thirties made two trips to Mexico.* Now she was determined to go to the other side of the world again, to a country where peace was not a dirty word: to India. Thanks to Wellington's generosity she would be able to go in style.

Mrs. Rankin was growing feebler; although her mind was still

* On a later visit to Mexico in the forties she rode a mule around the apex of the volcano Paricutin, in the state of Michoacán, which had recently erupted.

active, she could not get about because of rheumatism in her knees, and after one of her daughters devised a special wheelchair for her she never walked again. Eventually there were three nurses on duty to look after her, and every night to the nurse who put her to bed she would say cheerfully: "Good night, and if I don't see you in the morning, I'll see you in Heaven." Jeannette came to feel that her services were no longer needed, that she was merely a burden in her brother's house. In 1946, assured that Mrs. Rankin was in competent hands, she took off on her first trip to India by way of Turkey,* returning home after several months to spend the last winter of her mother's life with her in an apartment in Helena.

The passage to Turkey was made under circumstances that might have dampened the ardor of a less hardy traveler. Sailing on a former American troopship, the *Carp,* she found conditions on board so unsanitary, and the ship so unseaworthy, that 166 passengers were sick at one time: Equipped with what her friends called her "cast-iron stomach," Jeannette escaped the general malaise, and landed in Istanbul in high spirits. Here she visited with her friend Harriet Yarrow at the American University before making her way to India.

She was drawn to India as a country where a Jeannette Rankin might be welcomed, since it was the home of Gandhi, who had toppled a mighty empire through the power of passive resistance. Jeannette found Gandhi's message precisely applicable to her own beliefs. An interaction between Indian and American thought had begun more than a century earlier when Henry Thoreau, on taking out a membership in the Harvard Library, had drawn out as his first loan the sacred books of India. Reading such works as these brought Thoreau to his theory of civil disobedience, which in turn had prompted Gandhi to develop his theory of Satyagraha, a philosophy that enabled a whole people to change society by acting in defiance of unjust laws without violence. Jeannette was coming to the conclusion that these men had found the only way in which wars between nations could be

* At this time she was only sixty-six; she took her last trip to India when she was ninety.

avoided. In 1941, it will be remembered, she still believed that the United States should arm for defense, not realizing to what uses a "defense" establishment could be put. Now she was moving toward a belief in total universal disarmament, in the conviction that if you put a gun in a man's hand he will find some pretext to use it against his fellows.

During the next twenty years she made seven trips to India. On the first of these, traveling by boat, she brought her own car and debarked at Madras in the south, then proceeded to crisscross the subcontinent to get the feel of the country and its people. She was a fearless driver of long experience, inured to the hazards of the road, and her approach to simple people was so engaging that she could be assured of help whenever she needed it. Two months later she reached New Delhi, where she had been expected weeks earlier, the delay arousing some curiosity if not alarm among those who had been told to await her arrival. This initial visit came at a joyful time, when the first public meeting of the All-India Congress was held after the Congress leaders were released from jail. The Indians received her with honor, calling her "the Lady Rankin" because of her status as a former congressman. Jeannette had hoped to see Gandhi, who was then trying to bring Hindus and Moslems together to repair the damage of the communal riots, but on learning that he was getting up at four o'clock in the morning to walk a great distance to certain troubled areas, she decided not to ask for an interview at that time. The opportunity never came again, for Gandhi was assassinated the following year.

Her only contacts with the Indian leader were indirect; in 1952, on a trip to South Africa, she made the acquaintance of Gandhi's son, who had taken part in the passive resistance movement in Praetoria and the Transvaal under his father's direction; and on a previous visit to India to attend a meeting of the Women's International League for Peace and Freedom she spent four weeks at Gandhi's last ashram at Savagram, where his program was still observed. Here in a school he had established for basic education she found evidence of his intelligence at work. Jeannette had always been interested in educational methods, believing that the idea and ideal of peace should be instilled in children from their earliest years. At one time she had been attracted by the aims of Gundwig, a Dane who had set up what he called "folk schools"; and thanks to her friendship with Elisabeth Irwin, she was familiar with progressive movements in American education.

At Gandhi's ashram, however, she found what seemed to her the ideal teaching method, pervaded with the Gandhian spirit of mutual help and universal peace. In this school the children of Indian peasants learned their letters, their arithmetic, their science, their craft and their ethics at the same time. The teacher began by showing them the seed from which the cotton plant grew, and by recalling to them its cultivation on their family plots, she gave them lessons in husbandry and elementary botany; then she introduced them to the operations of carding, spinning, and finally weaving. At every step descriptive words were learned, so that language, spoken and written, was acquired along with the developing skill, while the mysteries of arithmetic were clarified by having the children run the school commissary. There were pitifully few objects in the schoolroom, but the origin, character and use of each one of them—the mats they sat on, the chalk or the blackboard, books or tools—became educational materials. Jeannette recalled that when the children sat at their spinning wheels they presented one of the most enchanting sights she had ever witnessed: their fingers and bodies moving like figures in a ballet to the hum of wheels and spindles.

In the course of her frequent travels in India she saw a great deal of the country and many different facets of life there. On her second trip she spent two weeks at Tagore's last home, and on another occasion she hired a car and chauffeur to drive her through states with which she was unfamiliar. In the course of this particular journey she picked up a hitchhiker who gave her a glimpse of problems and attitudes beyond the reach of the ordinary tourist. He was a tall, bearded young man wearing a huge turban, a Sikh, well educated, with charming manners. "I gave him a ride as far as he wanted to go," Jeannette told a friend later, so they had plenty of time for conversation, some of it quite harrowing, as their meeting took place soon after the Moslems had driven the Sikhs out of the Punjab. Not all Indians were as pacific as their dead leader, not even his successor, as she was to learn somewhat later.

On a subsequent trip to India she met the son of Nehru's doctor on the plane to Delhi, and through him she was able to arrange a meeting with the Prime Minister. Nehru received her with great courtesy, and they chatted amiably for a few moments, until Jeannette asked him about the role of Indian women in the independence movement. At this, she recalls, his face took on a distant look, and with reverence, almost in a trance, he told of their great deeds, much as he had described them in his autobiography. He spoke of how proud the political prisoners had been when they learned what the women had undertaken to do while their husbands and brothers and fathers were in jail; he spoke of his mother, his sisters and other relatives picketing the foreign cloth shops in the heat of the tropical sun; he told how his wife had thrown herself into organizing work despite ill health; he praised the courage with which they had accepted prison sentences. In his autobiography Nehru wrote that when his wife was questioned by a journalist at the time of her arrest she said that she was happy and proud to follow in the footsteps of her husband. "Probably she would not have said just that if she had thought over the matter," Nehru added, "for she considered herself a champion of woman's rights against the tyranny of man!"

The expression of such sentiments led Jeannette to believe that he was an enlightened leader. Meeting the Prime Minister soon afterward at a reception, she again found him very cordial, and attributed this to his sympathy with her views on peace. But on her next trip to India the situation had changed; the war against China in the Himalayas had begun, and Nehru showed himself to be as jingoistic as any flag-waving patrioteer. On the day she arrived in Delhi he had gone to Bombay to greet the navy, a gesture that showed how far he had departed from the Gandhian position. She did not try to renew the acquaintance.

Wherever she went she tried to observe the people, and if possible to communicate with them and serve them. In 1951 she wrote to Libby from aboard the *Ocean Mail* on her way to India that she had spent a few days in Japan. The Japanese, she said in her letter, were beginning to pick up loose ends and begin a new life with remarkable courage and patience.* Then she went on to say that her plans for India were not yet fixed. "One thing is certain," she wrote, ". . . there will be ample opportunity for growth, and I hope I shall come back better prepared to face our own problems." At the age of seventy-one she was still eager to learn and to use her knowledge in new ways.

Returning to New Delhi the following year, she was pleased to be able to welcome her sister Edna McKinnon and Margaret Sanger, who had come to India to attend an international congress on birth control. Edna recalls a hilarious episode during that visit, showing how outspoken Jeannette could be on occasion. While having breakfast at the hotel with the American delegation, all of whom were discussing the proposals to be put before the congress in the frankest terms, Jeannette suddenly rose to her feet. "All you talk about is vaginas, vaginas, vaginas," she exclaimed. "I'm getting out of here!"

A little later, however, she traveled with Edna to Uttar Pradesh, where they spent Christmas at Almora, within view of the Himalayas. Writing to Libby at about that time, she said nothing about the birth control congress but told him that she was doing a little social work in connection with a nursing home, "which brings me very close to all kinds of people."

During those wanderyears Jeannette's travels covered a large part of the world, taking her to Europe, Asia, Africa and South America. She used whatever transportation was available: ships (sometimes freighters), railroads, automobiles, buses, and, more frequently as time went on, planes. If camels had been necessary to bring her to a desired spot, no doubt she would have used them without hesitation. As her niece Dorothy Brown recalls:

> She would stay anywhere, without ever grumbling about accommodations or food, unless there wasn't any. I only heard her complain once: she had boarded a freighter for a six-week return from India, and no one aboard spoke English! Everyone at the Taj Mahal Hotel in Bombay knew and loved her; she

* Years later she told a friend that she could not bear to stay longer in Japan because of her sense of guilt with regard to the atomic bombs. "I was miserable there," she said.

would sit in the lobby enjoying political talk with any visitors as if it were her living room.

Once her plans were made, nothing could keep her at home but a crippling disability. "The Christmas of 1960," writes Dorothy Brown, "I put her on a plane for India, enveloped in a huge raincoat stuffed with bottles and bottles of aspirin for her tic douloureux." It was not until 1968 that she underwent an operation to relieve this painful malady.

One of the most ambitious of her voyages took place in 1962, when she was eighty-two years old. This astounding year started out with a flight to Ireland for a meeting with DeValera, whom she admired, and who no doubt admired her for her attempt to help Ireland win independence in 1918. She then went on to Helsinki, and from there to Leningrad, where she joined an American delegation led by Jerome Davis, who had come to Russia to attend the World Peace Congress held in Moscow that summer. Jeannette had asked to be allowed to travel with the American group, not as a delegate but as one dedicated to the peace movement who wanted to see how a Communist society worked. If she had tried to visit the Soviet Union on her own, the traveling arrangements would have been far more difficult.

She was greatly impressed by the efficient organization of the meetings in Moscow and was stirred by the repeated exhortations of the Russian leaders in favor of peace, but since she was not an official member of the American delegation, she was not invited to offer her own views on how peace could be achieved. The only chance she had to speak out was one she herself seized at a luncheon attended by some Russian dignitaries. Speaking for herself, she said, she favored immediate, total, unilateral disarmament by the United States. But there was no chance of attaining total disarmament in America, she added, because our country was controlled by the military. The Soviets, she said disingenuously, could decree immediate unilateral disarmament because they controlled their military! Her Russian hosts did not know what to make of this simplistic approach; in fact, no one had told them who she was and what gave her authority to speak in such a manner. Did she mean what she said, or was she being ironic, talking with tongue in cheek? Was this some sort of trap? Although they listened to her politely, they did not venture a reply; her American associates, on the other hand, seemed embarrassed, even disgruntled by her outburst. This was not the party line; it was the Jeannette Rankin line.

In addition to the stay in Moscow the group took in the usual sights and points of interest: theaters, museums, specimen factories, Leningrad, Yalta. Jeannette was interested to see that so many of the factory workers were women, including engineers and at least one very able plant manager. She made no attempt to break away from the prescribed itinerary, but enjoyed watching the people as they went about their work, and even more seeing them at play in the great public parks, drawing children to her with the American G.I.'s secret weapon, a copious supply of chewing gum. Finding herself seated beside a little boy in a theater in Leningrad, she ceremoniously exchanged gifts with him: she gave him a Lincoln penny and he gave her a little pin with a red star and a picture of Lenin on it.

After the visit to Russia her destination was Turkey, where she intended to stay once more with Harriet Yarrow at the American University, but as she was unable to make arrangements to travel there directly (even though she had been as far south in Russia as Yalta), she was obliged to go first to Poland. In Warsaw she had difficulties with her visa and would have been in a very awkward situation had not a West African black who had been studying medicine in England come to her rescue. Everyone she met was incredulous about her age; in the ladies' room at the airport in Turkey a young woman fell off her chair when she gathered—by sign language, no doubt—that Jeannette was eighty-two, old enough to be her great-grandmother. But with the exception of some bureaucratic officials she was always able to establish contact with people. In India, she has often said, she could always begin communicating with the native women by admiring their earrings. In Turkey, walking down the street one day she came on two women, one carrying a small baby, and immediately struck up a conversation of sorts. Within a few minutes the young mother had handed the baby over to the strange American and let her dandle it for a while. Jeannette's American friends were astounded by this incident, for before this no Turkish woman had been known to place such confidence in a foreigner.

Even after all this movement and wealth of impressions she was not yet ready to go home. Heading once more for India from Turkey, she traveled through Iran and Afghanistan and what is now Pakistan. It was probably on this trip that she visited Kashmir and indulged herself by living for a time in idle splendor on a houseboat afloat in the exquisite Wular Lake. Unspoiled by this pampered interval, she continued on her way to the heart of India and later joined Edna, who was doing family-planning work in Indonesia, where the housing and the climate offered few comforts.

She returned to America in high spirits and with no sign of fatigue. It had been an extraordinary odyssey, in particular for a woman of her age. Jeannette frequently remarked that she would never have enjoyed these far-flung journeys so much if she had been younger. On the one hand, travel involved no responsibility, and after decades of unceasing activity she had earned the right to a long vacation; on the other, she was no idle, gaping tourist, for her time was spent in constant study and observation of how other people lived, and wherever possible in spreading her gospel of peace. Nothing she encountered offered a challenge to her pacifist beliefs; indeed she was only confirmed in her principles by what she witnessed and experienced. If she, a woman of advanced years, a foreigner, ignorant of other languages and customs, could make friends in all nations, why couldn't those nations do the same?

Moreover, her exposure to the poverty, ignorance and injustice to be found everywhere gave force to her conviction that only in a world at peace could these problems be tackled with any prospect of success. People needed to be fed, housed, clothed, provided for in sickness and in old age; they needed education to be able to lead full lives and to learn to tolerate their neighbors; they needed to be dealt with fairly in order to deal fairly with others. Jeannette was not so simple as to suppose that the abolition of war would bring on the millennium; it would only be a beginning. As she approached her ninth decade, still an unregenerate pacifist, American military adventures in Southeast Asia had begun to arouse so much indignation among the people of the United States that her voice would again be heard in the land.

XI

Beginning Again

For twenty-five years after her second term in Congress none of Jeannette's activities brought her to public notice, with the result that in the nineteen-sixties many people, including earlier acquaintances, were not aware of the fact that she had survived. Others who met her for the first time during that period put her down as a harmless old lady. "She's no harmless little old lady," said Jeannette Mirsky, one of her old friends. "She's a ball of fire!" Miss Mirsky tells of a young man who had named his newly acquired Volkswagen "J.R." "It's named for Jeannette Rankin," he explained, "because I know it will *go*." For in 1967, when she was in her eighty-seventh year, Jeannette had once more begun to "go" after a quarter of a century of obscurity.

She had viewed the dispatch of the first American advisers to Vietnam in 1961 by President Kennedy with misgivings, which proved to be only too well justified when President Johnson sent large forces to Indochina and ordered the massive bombings that finally aroused the conscience of most Americans. In May 1967 she was asked to address a meeting in Atlanta at the home of Mrs. Nan Prendergast under the auspices of a group called Atlantans for Peace, one of hundreds of gatherings, teach-ins and other demonstrations staged that year to protest our involvement in

Southeast Asia. No more than a hundred persons were present when she gave her speech, but the gist of it was sent out over the Associated Press wires and made headlines throughout the country. Millions of Americans learned that the first woman member of Congress still lived, that she had voted against American engagement in two world wars, and that she had become more, not less, dedicated to pacifist principles. This speech was in fact the first widely publicized statement of her conversion to the ideas of Thoreau and Gandhi. "It is unconscionable," she said, "that 10,000 boys have died in Vietnam [at that time] and I predict that if 10,000 American women had mind enough they could end the war, if they were committed to the task, even if it meant going to jail."

Among the organizations planning to demonstrate against the war that year was a pacifist group called Women's Strike for Peace, whose western division, led by Vivian Hallinan, was working on a plan to dramatize the protest by a march on Washington to present a petition to Congress. At a meeting held in New York to coordinate the arrangements with women from other parts of the country, Clara DeMiha of the New York branch of the Women's Strike for Peace proposed that the marchers call themselves the Jeannette Rankin Brigade and that Jeannette be asked to head the procession. The suggestion was immediately adopted, indicating that there was still potency in the name. Mrs. Martin Luther King, Jr., a member of the organizing committee, issued a statement to the press which said: "She is the endurance symbol of the aspirations of American women—the symbol of the aspirations for peace of all of us." Jeannette was quick to accept the invitation, and a group of organizers went down to Georgia to see her about the arrangements.

The members of the committee who waited on her at "Shady Grove" were both startled and charmed by the bizarre domain of this world-famous old woman. They found her in residence at a modest cottage (formerly a sharecropper's shanty) set low in a grove of trees, not far from a more modern house occupied by a black family, the Wonder Robinsons, with a curious round building on an elevation about a hundred yards away. Wonder

Robinson did the heavier chores around the place, trimming the lawn, picking up wood for the fire, and looking after simple repairs, while his wife Mattie did occasional cleaning and laundering for Jeannette. During her absence elsewhere, Wonder acted as caretaker, and Jeannette used to tell with a chuckle that she always found her house in order when she returned because she gave him an extra bonus if no one had broken in while she was away. The Robinson children looked on her with awe, but also with the deepest love and trust.*

The houses were islands in a sea of creepers, one of which, the kudzu, was so parasitic that it tended to encroach on the cleared space and strangle the nearby trees. Since it was also a hiding place for poisonous snakes, it needed to be cut away and "rolled up" periodically. This was a task that Jeannette used to superintend, while the children helped, despite their terror of the snakes. One day one of them asked in disbelief, "Miss Rankin, ain't you afraid of nothing?" When she shook her head he went back to work with more confidence.

Jeannette's house consisted of four fairly large rooms, more ample living space than she had had in Bogart, and with a few more sybaritic features. It was apparent to her visitors that she measured every "modern improvement" against a possible loss of her independence. As a concession to her advancing years she had had electricity installed, which freed her from the trouble and danger of oil lamps, as well as allowing for the acquisition of an electric hot plate, frypan, heater, and electric blankets. One of the rooms, on a lower level, had a rammed earth floor covered with Oriental rugs, gifts from her family or purchases made on her travels, which provided a silent and pleasing surface

* Tacked up on her bedroom wall Jeannette kept a letter that little Jennifer Robinson, aged eleven, wrote her one day:

> Dear Jennette Rankin
> You is coming home tonight I did miss you and I no you miss me Stanley Wonder and Mattie Jeff and me miss you We wrote you a letter did you Right us a letter We send you some picture and we send you a letter Miss Rankin I did miss you I love you all of us Love you
> from Jennifer
> Love you

to walk on.* The living room was heated by a huge fieldstone fireplace fed by fallen branches or by the Sunday edition of the *New York Times* set up on a rack of her own invention.

In recent years she had made two other concessions to modernity: water had been piped into the house, and a toilet and tub installed, but since she had not got around to acquiring a pump, the toilet was flushed from a tall tin jug filled at the single water tap in the bath. Hot water for bathing was furnished by a kettle on the big old-fashioned stove in the kitchen. For a cup of tea or coffee she used an odd electric device she had found in India, which when submerged in cold water heated it to the boiling point in less than a minute. (It had to be handled with care, to avoid a short circuit or an electric shock.) When asked whether she ever considered further modernization of her home, Jeannette used to say that she preferred to spend her money on her travels; at other times she maintained that whatever she could spare above her living costs went for the peace movement or other causes in which she was interested. Wellington had in fact provided for her needs adequately some years earlier by giving her a ranch from which she drew a regular income. And when he died in 1966 he left her enough money to buy a retirement home in Carmel, California, where she usually spent the winters. The idea of "retirement" was very distasteful to her, and she only succumbed to the proposal under family pressure, preferring the informality of her Georgia cottage, with all its inconveniences, to the beautifully appointed studio apartment at the Carmel Valley Manor, sometimes referring to it as her "death house."

The visitors from Women's Strike for Peace were especially curious about the round house on the hill which struck such an odd note in the Georgia landscape. The round house was in effect Jeannette's folly, one of the few ventures she ever embarked upon that had brought no returns, either practically or morally. She was inspired to have it built in the middle sixties, after returning from the Orient by boat in the company of half

* Jeannette had always been interested in rammed earth houses, and after her house in Bogart burned down, she had got local help to put up a small building of this type of construction where the kitchen once stood, but it was never completed by her after she bought the Watkinsville house.

a dozen women of retirement age—a long voyage that she expected would be at best tiresome, at worst dismal. To her surprise, her fellow voyagers proved to be amiable, lively, self-sufficient and mutually helpful, not a clutch of old biddies full of self-pity. This experience had given her the notion that older women living alone, or under sufferance with relatives, might make interesting lives for themselves if they came together in a kind of commune, where they could share some of their activities and yet retain a degree of privacy. The women she had in mind would be of limited means, not in a position to travel at will or take up residence in an elegant senior citizens' development. If the scheme worked out well, she saw no reason why it could not be copied all over the country, providing a purposeful way of life for a segment of the population in whom no one took any interest.

On her return to Georgia, therefore, she designed a building to be made of cement blocks, in form resembling the round stone barn of the Shakers (which she had never seen), consisting of a large central atriumlike room lit by clerestory windows with ten wedge-shaped sleeping chambers surrounding it. Her plans, which called for cooking facilities in the common room, and three bathrooms to one side, were approved by the local building commissioners save for the bathroom feature. The commissioners maintained that there should be a bathroom attached to each bedroom in order to save water, and it took no little explaining on Jeannette's part to convince them that ten women using three bathrooms would draw no more water than if they had ten bathrooms.

The building completed, she looked about for applicants to occupy what one member of the visiting committee called "a kibbutz, Georgia style." But there were no takers. The women she expected to come forward to join in the communal experiment evidently preferred the discomforts of a situation to which they were accustomed to an arrangement with so many incommensurable features. The round house stood idle for many months, an attraction to curiosity seekers and a source of chagrin to Jeannette, until one day some youths from a fraternity at the nearby University of Georgia turned up to ask if they could rent it for a month, with the possibility of a longer lease. Jeannette consented, happy to have young people near her. The young men drove out one afternoon, held a wild party that lasted through the night, and departed the next morning, never to return. After another period of idleness the round house briefly sheltered some hippies who were soon evicted by the police for possession of drugs, a charge Jeannette believed was concocted to rid the neighborhood of the longhairs. In the end the investment of both time and money was a total loss for Jeannette save for one thing: it reminded her that she operated best in the areas that she knew and cared for most.* The invitation to take a leading part in the antiwar protest by a march on Washington was just what she needed to erase the memory of her disappointment and to restore her faith in herself. After so many years during which the pacifist cause had been dormant, she hoped that there was now an opportunity to review and revive the traditions of the peace movement, not only to stop the current war but to prevent all future wars.

The day chosen for the march of the Jeannette Rankin Brigade was January 15, 1968, the date of the opening of the last session of Congress in President Johnson's administration. As originally planned, the women were to assemble at the Union Station and then to proceed across the square to the Capitol steps, where a delegation would present petitions calling for an end to the war to congressional leaders, in full view of the demonstrators. These arrangements, however, were vetoed by the Capitol police, who claimed that they were in violation of section 193(g) of Title 40 of the United States Code, which read that it was forbidden "to parade, stand, or move in processions or assemblages in said United States Capitol Grounds." Only small groups of ten to fifteen persons would be allowed to gather at the Capitol steps, as ordinary visitors. Organizers of the Jeannette Rankin Brigade went to court to seek an injunction against this ruling as being in

* It is evident from the terms of her will, however, that she continued to entertain hopes for the project. One clause reads: ". . . five acres of said land surrounding the round house for women workers and the house shall be distributed to such charitable foundation as shall be selected by my Executrix, to be used for the benefit of unemployed women workers as a home. . . ."

Members of the Jeannette Rankin Brigade, with Miss Rankin in the center wearing glasses, as they marched from Union Station to the Capitol in January 1968. Several thousand women marched.

United Press International Photo

violation of the First Amendment to the Constitution, but they were unsuccessful.*

The marchers were therefore rerouted from the station through the park and around to the rear of the Capitol along a path prescribed by the police. Five thousand women (by the police count; ten thousand by the count of some experienced reporters) from all over the United States had put aside their duties

* With the assistance of the New Jersey Civil Liberties Union the Jeannette Rankin Brigade appealed this decision, asking to have section 193(g) declared unconstitutional. On May 9, 1972, the U.S. District Court for the District of Columbia found in their favor, and on November 6, 1972, the Supreme Court affirmed the decision. It is now possible to hold demonstrations of any size which are conducted peacefully and do not interfere with the conduct of congressional business on the Capitol grounds.

at home to take part in the demonstration. The scene: overcast skies, a solemn defile of women clad in mourning, marching to no music, with here and there an older woman in a wheelchair, or a young mother pushing a child in a stroller. Jeannette led the way until she turned off with a few others to go directly to the Capitol. The law-and-order forces were on their best behavior, suggesting that the administration was hesitant to risk unfavorable publicity if heads were cracked and jails crowded. A policeman held Jeannette's arm in friendly fashion, and when one of her friends objected, saying, "She can walk. You don't need to help her," he replied gallantly: "Don't deprive me of that pleasure." Jeannette herself could not refrain from taking a fling at her "protector." "You don't need to worry about us," she said. "We are unarmed and not at all threatening. Do you really need those great big guns to handle an old lady?"

She was permitted to lead a group of sixteen women, among them Mrs. Martin Luther King, Jr., into the Capitol building to present a petition to Speaker McCormack on behalf of the Women's Strike for Peace. The petition urged that Congress (1) resolve to end the war in Southeast Asia and withdraw all American troops from Vietnam; (2) use its power to heal a sick society at home; (3) use its power to make reparations for the ravaged land in Vietnam; and (4) listen to what the American people were saying and refuse the insatiable demands of the military-industrial complex. Speaker McCormack received the ladies, took the petition, and went back to what no doubt he deemed more important business.

The sixteen women then walked to the office of Senator Mike Mansfield, where only Jeannette, Edna McKinnon, Dorothy Brown and one other person from Montana were admitted, on the ground that the Senator was receiving only constituents. Mansfield evidently intended to make the meeting more of a social occasion than a political confrontation, for he had the tea table all set for his visitors. Jeannette refused to fall into his trap; she talked so much and so fast, she reported later, that he had no time to serve up his little collation. As she left the Capitol grounds reporters asked her about her reception by the Senator from Montana. She replied that he might have received a larger delegation without personal danger. "He was not so brave," she

As leader of the Jeannette Rankin Brigade March on Washington in January 1968 to protest the war in Vietnam, Miss Rankin presents a petition to Senator Mike Mansfield. On the left are her sister Edna McKinnon and her niece Dorothy McKinnon Brown.

said. "He had all the police and guards to protect him. There is no reason why old ladies shouldn't be allowed to go into the Capitol."

When the delegation returned to the paraders assembled behind the Capitol grounds, the women all got into buses and were driven to the Shoreham Hotel, where Jeannette, still lively after a day of facing up to policemen, congressmen and reporters (and one hour with a radio interviewer), gave a stirring speech that was received with enthusiasm.

Once more she was back in her element as a leader and a spokesman for humane values, roles she was not to relinquish for the rest of her life. From that time forward she took part in many peace demonstrations, including marches both in Georgia and in California; in 1971 she was photographed licking envelopes in a letter campaign directed to the President which was sponsored by a group called "Another Mother and Others for Peace."

The truth is that Jeannette was getting on in years, although she would not admit that this was any reason to curtail her activities. Like anybody else, she was subject to various bodily ailments, but she tended to be secretive about them; they either passed away or were borne with fortitude. Her heart and will were still strong and active, and as she approached her tenth decade she was determined to resume her travels to far places. Meanwhile, in celebration of her ninetieth birthday on June 11, 1970, her friends planned to do her honor with a great dinner in Washington, but before this was to take place she made up her mind to go off on another trip to Russia, which she had seen only sketchily on her previous visit and where she hoped to be able to measure peace sentiment more accurately than before. All the arrangements for this tour were completed when she went into the village of Watkinsville one day in March and fell down on the steps in front of the local drugstore.

A man standing nearby rushed over to help her up. "Don't touch me," she said calmly. Another man, and another, and another, joined the first, but until there were six of them she refused all aid. She knew that she had broken her hip, and that if she were improperly handled the consequences might be permanently crippling. A call was sent in to her good friend Ted Harris, the local minister, who came immediately with his wife and saw her safely to the hospital, staying there through the night until all the proper measures were taken. Before she was carried off by the Harrises, one of the bystanders saw a curious object lying on the ground. He eyed it mistrustfully. "What's this?" he asked, prodding it with his foot. "That's my wig," said Jeannette. "Give it to me."*

The trip to Russia had to be called off, of course, or perhaps in Jeannette's mind merely put off until later. A hip fracture in a person of her age generally puts an end to an active life; the victim is expected to accept invalidism for the rest of her days. Jeannette Rankin was of another fiber; she put as much effort into her recovery as she had put into any of her other projects. Within a month she was using a walker to get about hospital corridors, for, as she explained to her friends and family, she

* Her hair having turned white when she was thirty-five, she had for many years had it tinted, but occasionally an inexpert coiffeur gave it so singular a color that when the fashion for wigs returned she resorted to it gratefully.

On her ninetieth birthday, June 11, 1970, celebrated by a dinner at the Rayburn House Office Building in Washington.

United Press International Photo

wanted to be able to get to her birthday dinner on her own two feet. Pain was something she rarely mentioned, and it was difficult to tell whether she had a very high pain threshold or whether in accordance with deeply ingrained habit she had already dismissed her present suffering and was planning for the future.

Yet, for all her determination, she was obliged to use a wheelchair to arrive at the reception and dinner at the Rayburn House Office Building on June 11, 1970. Her eyes brilliant, her face glowing, she sat on the dais flanked by Senators Mike Mansfield and Lee Metcalf of Montana, men who had begun their political careers as representatives from the First District, from which she had been elected in 1940. Among other dignitaries at the high table were Congressman Arnold Olsen of Montana, the current incumbent from the First District, Senator Margaret Chase Smith of Maine, Representative Patsy Mink of Hawaii, former Senators Gerald P. Nye, Burton K. Wheeler and Ernest Gruening, while scattered through the banquet room were former associates, leaders in the peace movement, members of her family, and more than a hundred friends of all ages and occupations.

As was to be expected on such an occasion, the speakers of the evening paid handsome tribute to Jeannette for her stand against war, so apposite to the conflict currently raging in Southeast Asia with increasing ferocity. Leading off, Senator Mansfield, after a few compliments, expressed his own frustration when he said: "Jeannette, the difference between your day and ours is that in your day they used to give Congress a chance to declare wars." And Senator Smith, who followed Mansfield, credited Jeannette with having had an important influence on her own career. Only a few days earlier there had been a lively debate on Capitol Hill on the Byrd amendment, which would have authorized President Nixon to send United States troops back into Cambodia without seeking advance consent of Congress. The amendment had been defeated, and Senator Smith was among those voting against it. For this, she said, she owed Jeannette Rankin a large debt.

> She broke the way for me by being elected in 1916. I salute her for being the original dove in Congress. Senate doves shot down the Byrd amendment. Even I voted against it. Perhaps it was Miss Rankin's influence on such a stubborn hawk as I have been known to be.

It was Lee Metcalf, the junior senator from Montana, however, who went into specifics and gave a picture of Jeannette's career in depth, stressing the contemporaneity of the issues for which she had given battle. "We honor tonight a woman young in heart," he began, "who not only has survived a generation gap but has jumped over a couple of generations and is now shoulder to shoulder with the youngsters of today who are seeking peace." And then he listed the causes with which she had identified herself:

> She spoke for child welfare, of industrial and labor problems, of economic maladjustments . . . the interdependence of all nations in distribution of the world's goods, the pressure of growing populations, social injustice, racial prejudice. She believed in freedom for our First American—the American Indian—and of his needs for education and recognition. She was in-

> terested in the development of public lands, including our public parks. . . . These all sound like a reading of the calendar of issues before Congress today.

He then went on to catalogue legislation she had proposed that was now part of the body of American law:

> suffrage for women, support for dependents of enlisted men, free postage for members of the armed forces, granting to American women married to aliens the right to retain their citizenship, creation of a water-power board. . . . She is . . . a saver with a great heart, a builder, a trail-blazer and an example to all legislators who would have the courage of their convictions. I salute Jeannette Rankin for her effective interest in Western problems that have influenced global civilization. It was easier to represent the First District of Montana independently because of her example.

Most of the speakers read their tributes from a prepared text, but when it came time for Jeannette to make acknowledgment, she used neither script nor notes. Rising from her wheelchair, she presented a figure of timeless elegance, dressed as she was in a costume of her own design made in India of gold-tinted silk. At a distance her face showed astonishingly few lines, and her eyes, despite an operation for tic douloureux that affected the musculature of one of them, retained much of the expressive look of her youth. She had lost but little of her clear articulation and suffered only slightly from the forgetfulness of many persons of her age, fumbling occasionally for a word or a name but almost never for a fact or a relevant anecdote.

Beginning with a brief reference to her recent accident, she made an observation with symbolic overtones: On arriving at the airport the preceding day she had been astonished to see that all the people bustling about had two legs and could walk—not only the men but also the women!

And now she departed from the customary generalities of such speeches by projecting new fields of action. Granted that the occasion was a milestone, she would not accept it as a valedictory. It was not to be assumed that she was finished, that her career was over. She had a platform, she had a thesis, and she meant to speak out. As her niece, Mrs. Mary Elizabeth Huber, remarked

Miss Rankin sends a letter to President Nixon in 1971, urging him to stop the war in Vietnam.

afterward, all the other speakers had described her past achievements, while Jeannette alone addressed herself to the future. Her ideal, she said, was the broadest possible extension of the democratic process to achieve peace. She offered two concrete proposals for the modification of the American political system to bring this about: the direct election of the President by preferential vote; and the multiple-member district for representatives in Congress. The first would give the electorate a real choice among various candidates, instead of a choice between two persons selected by others. The second would provide representation for differing points of view at the district level.

Through giving democracy the broadest base, she maintained, by making officeholders responsive to the deepest needs and longings of the people, world peace could be attained. For her greatest concern was to put an end to all wars, and, most immediately, to put an end to the war in Vietnam. War is a habit, she said, repeating her old slogan, and we must make up our minds to change the habit. To begin with, we must stop preparing for war, for whenever an emergency arises, we think it can be settled by war. But if the United States, the biggest and strongest nation in the world, decided to lay down its arms and resolved not to have recourse to wars, every nation in the world would have to do the same, because all other nations were arming out of uncertainty as to which side the United States would take in a crisis. "We'd be the safest country in the world if the world knew that we didn't have a gun," she said. "Men are not killed," she concluded, "because they get mad at each other. They're killed because one of them has a gun in any dispute."

A guest at the banquet could not gauge how much of the applause that followed her speech was a mark of esteem for the guest of honor and how much was acceptance of her thesis. No matter. As long as she had breath, Jeannette Rankin intended to offer her simple, rational arguments on how to win the world for peace. The dinner came to a close with a champagne toast and a rush up to the dais for handshaking and autographs. The fete was over, but for her there was still work to be done.

XII

Forever Young

There is only one solution if old age is not to be an absurd parody of our former life, and that is to go on pursuing ends that give our existence a meaning—devotion to individuals, to groups or causes, social, political, intellectual or creative work. One's life has value so long as one attributes value to the life of others, by means of love, friendship, indignation, compassion.
Simone de Beauvoir

In our time Picasso and George Bernard Shaw and Lord Russell have been outstanding examples of what de Beauvoir meant by her advice to the aging; another is Jeannette Rankin, who seemed to be continually renewed and freshened by every challenge as the decades rolled by. Now that she had become newsworthy once more, her views on current issues were sought by all the media, and she did not hesitate to respond, speaking not as an elder statesman but as a contemporary in spirit of all the rebellious groups of the time. The women activists, most of whom had known her only as a name in the history books, claimed her as their own. No one knew better than she how the feminist movement of the early years of the century had been rechanneled and blocked after suffrage was won.

An old pro in dealing with the press, she had an apt, quotable answer to every question. Speaking to a reporter from the *Washington Post* on her ninetieth birthday, she granted that the women's liberation movement was doing splendid work. "But I can't get excited about it because I got so excited so long ago. . . . Everything they talk about now [abortion, etc.] we talked about before 1914." She urged that women be paid to take care of their children, "because most women would prefer to stay home with their children" rather than do less rewarding work elsewhere in order to pay for a housekeeper. She said that equal pay for equal work was only a superficial solution. "What we need is a complete revision of the monetary system." She owned up to a certain impatience with far-out demonstrations by women's lib groups, but maintained that they would cease "once people get the idea that women are human beings. And that will come when women behave like human beings and stop submitting to everything and everyone."

As an example of how women knuckled under to men, she told another journalist that women who consented to having their sons drafted reminded her of cows on the ranch: "A cow has a calf and after a while some man comes along and takes the calf away. She bawls for a while, then goes on and has another calf." There were penalties for women who chose the road of protest, she said to a reporter from a Tacoma newspaper: "If they're independent, talkative, and say what they think, they can't get a job or a husband. Look at me—unmarried and unemployed most of my life!" It was woman's responsibility to free herself, not wait for freedom to be granted to her.

When questioned about race relations, she drew the parallel with the feminist movement: "There has never been an argument advanced against Negroes which was not first used against women." And in another interview she took a stand that was also stressed by Shirley Chisholm, Bella Abzug, and others in the Women's Political Caucus: that there should be more women in public office. "We're half the people; we should be half the Congress," she said.

Her views on the war in Vietnam were also solicited, and her answers were no less forthright than on the woman question. A reporter from the *San Francisco Examiner* quoted her as saying:

"War is nonsense—bring the boys back forthwith." When it was suggested to her that this might be interpreted as surrender, she answered: "Surrender is a military idea. When you're doing something wrong, you stop." The Vietnam war, she held, was a unilateral war, and with a unilateral war you can have a unilateral peace. "There's nothing to keep us from saying that we've run out of surplus war material and it's time to pack up and go home," she said in another interview. But how were we to get the boys home? she was asked on another occasion. "The same way we got them in, by ships and planes." She was not alarmed by campus violence, she told a reporter from the *St. Louis Post-Dispatch*. "If a nation sends boys halfway around the world to be shot, can you blame a few little boys for throwing stones?"

In her speeches at the time she drew on her great fund of anecdotes, some of them earthy in the style of her old friend Chic Sale. One of these was designed to illustrate her theory that the country would be safe from foreign attack even without defense installations. A countryman went into a bar one day, she told, and, after drinking several beers, asked to be directed to the toilet. The bartender handed him a key, which the man accepted with wonder. "We had an unlocked outhouse on our farm where I lived for twenty years," he exclaimed, "and in all that time no one ever stole a single, tiny turd!"

This kind of plain speaking, this homely American wit about problems of the greatest moment, is quite refreshing to many people; on the other hand, it is dismissed as shallow by those who believe that Jeannette was not "realistic," not a profound thinker. Among those who agree with her that it is woman's responsibility to free herself from all forms of servitude, there are some who will not grant that it is the responsibility of all human beings to free themselves from war, another form of servitude. In reality, for many years Jeannette had been giving a great deal of thought to how this other liberation could be attained. To her mind people everywhere were overwhelmingly against war; they were led into battle primarily because the political system did not allow them to express their views directly, and secondarily because governments misled them as to the issues involved.

Although many of her ideas were unorthodox, Jeannette was

no revolutionary, either Communist or anarchist; she was on the contrary firmly committed to the principles of democracy and free elections that reflect the people's choice. What she sought to overcome was the rigidity of political structures and party infrastructures that blocks a truly democratic expression of the people's will. To make government responsive, she believed, it was necessary to revise our election procedures. In her birthday speech she had referred to two remedies which she had been formulating for some time, remedies which could clear the arteries of the body politic and keep the blood of public opinion flowing freely up to the highest echelons of government. From now on she was to give herself over to a one-man campaign to win acceptance of these two proposals: direct popular election of the President by preferential vote; and multimember district representation in Congress.

In her Carnegie Hall speech as long ago as 1917, before she went to Congress for the first time, she had called for the direct election of the President, a belief shared by many reformers of the time who looked on the Electoral College as an anachronism. But the proposal needed sharper definition, for the direct election of the President would not be truly representative of the people's choice if they were offered, as before, only two candidates from whom to choose, two candidates with enough support from party hacks and enough funds to win the nomination. The solution to this, Jeannette held, was a greatly enlarged list of candidates, for whom the voters could indicate their choice in order of preference. Thus if the voter's first choice lost out, his vote would count toward his second choice; if his second choice did not poll a majority, his vote would count toward a third choice, and so on.

For many years the mechanics of direct preferential voting in so large a country seemed an insuperable obstacle to the realization of her scheme, until the electronic age following World War II cleared the way and giant computers came into use. She now saw that the optical character recognition machines adopted by the Social Security Administration could be used to count the vote. The time needed for tabulating the vote would be shortened; great savings could be made by doing away with primaries and run-offs; and the public would be able to express an opinion on issues rather than choose between Tweedledum and Tweedledee.

Already in 1969 she had begun her campaign by circulating a leaflet entitled "Case for a Direct Preferential Vote" in which she stated her arguments very persuasively. "Without free choice of candidates," the leaflet read, "voting becomes an empty act, a meaningless mass ritual of acceptance and conformity." Realizing nonetheless that parts of her plan might be obscure, she called for widespread discussion of the whole idea as well as of details of its implementation. At that very time the Senate Subcommittee on Constitutional Amendments under the chairmanship of Senator Birch Bayh was holding hearings on an amendment to the Constitution providing for the direct election of the President, and Jeannette wrote to a friend in October that she was "on her way to Washington to educate the Congress on a preferential vote." Gladys McKenzie, who was present at the hearing, described the scene when Jeannette came to give her testimony. As she entered the committee room, men rushed forward to help the venerable old lady to her seat. She brushed them aside. The chairman said that she might remain seated while addressing the committee members. "May I stand?" she asked. "I fight better when I'm standing up."*

The committee members did not act on her suggestion, but Jeannette was not discouraged. In every speech she gave thereafter she made a plea for the preferential vote. She knew that great changes were not wrought overnight, but she had great faith in the seminal value of a progressive idea.

She conducted a similar campaign for her second plan for the extension of the democratic process: multiple-member district representation in Congress. The value of this had been apparent to her as far back as 1916, when she ran for Congress the first time. Montana then had so small a population that it was not divided into congressional districts but was represented by two congressmen-at-large. Her victory then, she believed, was due to the support she drew not from a delimited area but from all over

* William Fitts Ryan, the late congressman from New York, also attended the hearing and said to her when she had finished her testimony: "Thank you for coming and getting us to think about the unthinkable."

the state. She won the vote of those who favored woman suffrage, while those who opposed women in office voted for the Democratic candidate. Both points of view were thus represented. Her theory gained credibility when Montana was divided into two districts, which the legislature gerrymandered expressly to assure her defeat in case she tried to run again in 1918.

Single-member districting, she pointed out, had the disadvantage of permitting only one congressman, "with a single set of ideas," to represent a district where there may be several different points of view. Under the present system those different points of view go unrepresented, whereas her plan would provide for a broad spectrum of political beliefs and social attitudes. As in the case of her scheme for a direct preferential presidential election, she urged multiple-member districting in all her speeches, wrote out summaries of how it would work, and distributed these to political figures and others who might be interested. In the autumn of 1971 she presented her summary to the Georgia legislature; in March 1972 she offered it for consideration to the Montana Constitutional Convention, not in expectation of immediate adoption but in the hope of stimulating the widest possible discussion.

At ninety-one her carriage was as erect as ever. The hip fracture did not make her lame, but it had left her a bit timid, and she had come to use a cane, emphasizing to her friends that it was needed not for support but merely to give her confidence on unfamiliar terrain, for she did not like to admit that her eyes were not so sharp as they had been. She took pride in being able to live alone in Georgia, but in reality she was seldom without company. The Robinsons were there to run errands, and house guests turned up frequently to enjoy the old Rankin hospitality. But what made life in Georgia so agreeable to her was a group of devoted younger friends who out of love and respect for her mission assisted her in her projects and watched over her welfare constantly. One of these was Reita Rivers of Athens, who in addition to other services gave what time she could spare from her own work at the university to type Jeannette's letters and keep track of her appointments. Blanche Butler, daughter of a farmer in the neighborhood, who had known Jeannette first when a little girl, bringing her eggs, milk and vegetables, now married and with a family, provided her old friend with one delicious hot meal a day either in her own home or at Shady Grove if Jeannette was not well enough to come out. Ted Harris, minister of the Universalist church in Watkinsville, and his wife Jean were always on hand for useful offices. There were many others in the vicinity who could be called on when she needed help of one kind or another.

In 1971, however, she acquired an assistant who gradually took charge of all her arrangements for public appearances and at the same time took on many of the household chores. John Kirkley, a young law student, roared up to the cottage on his motorcycle one day to make Jeannette's acquaintance, and soon took up residence in her attic room. A vegetarian, Kirkley was a good cook, specializing in health foods; he wrote well and typed expertly; he was sympathetic to Jeannette's views on war and showed a quick grasp of her latest proposals for broader democratization of the political system. He encouraged her to keep going, to make herself heard, to respond to every invitation for a public appearance and seek out others. He would be her secretary and her manager—her impresario in a way; he would see to her transportation and food and lodging on all her stops.

Jeannette responded to this stimulus like Sarah Bernhardt on one of her farewell tours. She took John up on his challenge and once more went back on the road, a traveling salesman for peace and democracy, journeying north, east and west across the country, attending and speaking at meetings, regional conferences, women's caucuses, dinner gatherings, and what provided an even larger audience, on radio and television programs with nationwide coverage. The program of three months' activities in 1972 shows Jeannette Rankin at the age of ninety-two moving at almost the same velocity as Jeannette Rankin at thirty-six when running for Congress.

Leaving Georgia on Sunday, January 16, after being interviewed at the airport by Jo Ann Edgar of *Ms.* magazine, she flew into New York to stay with Gloria Steinem, with whom she was to appear on the David Frost television show. On Tuesday she taped her part of the Frost show with Steinem, dealing with all the subjects of her concern: feminism, peace, reform of the political system.*

On Wednesday she was interviewed by Nadine Brozan of the *New York Times* whose article, published on January 24, gave a vivid picture of the spirited old fighter. When Brozan asked her what she would do if she had her life to live over again, she said that she wouldn't do anything differently, with one exception. "This time," she answered promptly, "I'd be nastier."

She was getting into her stride now. Returning to Georgia, on February 4 she took part in the initiation of Shirley Chisholm's campaign for the presidency in Atlanta, speaking briefly at a banquet held that evening. On February 12 she drove to Nashville, Tennessee, where she was interviewed by newspaper, radio and television reporters on her arrival. At 9:30 the next morning she gave the principal address at the Southern Women's Conference for Delegate Selection, a nonpartisan group which was working to get more women delegates at the two presidential conventions.

This was just the beginning of her day. Emplaning for New York around noon, she put up at the Hotel Commodore, where the regional conference of the National Organization for Women (NOW) was being held. NOW had named Jeannette as the first member of the 'Susan B. Anthony Hall of Fame," an honor to be awarded annually to living women who had made a notable contribution to women's rights. As the presentation ceremonies were not to take place until late in the afternoon, Jeannette was able to rest for a few hours before making her appearance. At 6:30 she walked in briskly, with no sign of fatigue after her strenuous program. The audience, consisting mainly of young people, seemed to catch its breath: Was this elegant, erect little woman the formidable Jeannette Rankin who had fought for women's rights and for peace before they or their parents were born? The applause was spontaneous and pro-

* An old trouper, she was extremely sensitive to the impression she made on an audience. Some months earlier she had been on the Merv Griffin show as one of a panel of ancient relics of the thirties, several of whom had maundered along at such length that she had no time to speak of current issues. After that experience she insisted on taped or live interviews with only one or at most two persons, which enabled her to appear as a contemporary activist, not a well-preserved antique.

Named as the first member of the Susan B. Anthony Hall of Fame, January 1971.

Michael Oreskes

longed; the faces turned to her were filled with love and recognition. Blinded by a sudden rush of tears, for a moment Jeannette felt she would not be able to say a word. Later she admitted to a friend that not in half a century had she been so deeply moved on a public platform.

Then she launched into one of the most cogent, well-expressed speeches she had given in many years: a projection of future tasks, and a summing up of her own life's work. She had been named for the Susan B. Anthony Hall of Fame as "the world's outstanding living feminist," she said, and she could only affirm her solidarity with the women of today who once more were seeking to achieve those goals. The number of young people in the audience was especially heartening to her, for she could see that they were prepared and determined to carry on the struggle.

> Women must devote all their energies today in gaining enough political offices to influence the direction of government away from the military-industrial complex and toward solving the major social disgraces that exist in our country. . . . We are here together to work together for the elimination of war. . . . My dream has always been that women would take this re-

> sponsibility. . . . We have to gather women from every walk of life, starting with the precinct.

And reminding her listeners of the battle for woman suffrage in the early years of the century, she described the techniques that had finally brought victory:

> We divided everybody into three categories: those who were with us, those who were against us, and the undecided. We didn't bother with the converted; we put them to work for us; and we didn't bother with the opposition; we concentrated on the undecided. And you must do the same. Make Congress more representative of the people. We worked hard for the right to vote. Now we need to work hard for someone to vote for. . . . We cannot progress unless we abolish the war system and work for a better participatory democracy for the betterment of mankind.

The speech, the speaker, the occasion itself, all made a powerful impression on more than one present. In times like these, when many young people have rejected the very idea of past history, denying its usefulness to explain present evils and present aspirations, Jeannette was a phenomenon new to their experience. Older people were assumed to be conservative, however radical they had been in their youth, timid about change, blind to injustice. But here was a woman out of that despised past, a woman who had been on the barricades long ago and was ready to join them on their newly erected barricades; here she was in the flesh with her words of wise counsel and encouragement, bidding them to dare greatly and go further even than she had been able to go. She was a living link not only with the feminists of her own generation but also with all those of more remote ages who had worked to remedy the human condition.

Her warm reception gave her the strength later that same evening to join a group from the NOW conference in a walk across town to Times Square, where they placed a papier-mâché bust of Susan B. Anthony (The Mother of Us All) on top of the statue of Father Duffy, the famous World War I chaplain. And still lively the next morning, she came down from her room at the Commodore to attend other meetings of the regional conference, at which Shirley Chisholm, Bella Abzug and Betty Friedan spoke. On the following Wednesday she went uptown to Barnard College to speak at the Women's Center and have lunch with the director; after lunch she gave an interview to Elizabeth Frappolo of *Life* magazine.

Then back she went to Georgia for a short rest, after which she was driven to Atlanta to give the opening address at the Georgia Women's Political Caucus. The main theme of her speech here was the direct election of the president by preferential vote, and to prove the feasibility of her plan she distributed sample ballots to the audience, along with instructions on how to use them. The interest shown was very gratifying. Off again in the afternoon for New York, she gave a talk at the Fourth Annual Meeting of the Jeannette Rankin Brigade Rank-and-File at the Ethical Culture Auditorium. The next day, March 6, she taped a radio interview for the "Today's Woman" program.

On March 7 she flew to Helena to be present at meetings of the Montana Constitutional Convention, which was debating the extension of the ballot to persons over the age of eighteen. This was a festive homecoming, visiting with relatives and attending receptions, at which she shared the honors with John Gardner of Common Cause. Along with Gardner, she had been named as one of the distinguished visitors to the convention, and in that role she was invited to give the last speech of the occasion on March 14, in the very chamber where she had addressed the legislature on the suffrage issue in 1911. But now she was no timid suppliant; she spoke with confidence and authority.

Early in her discourse she tried to make the Montanans aware of the dangers that surrounded them because of the country's military orientation. In the eyes of the national leadership, she pointed out, the population of Montana was considered "expendable," since the hundreds of missile silos buried there placed the state in the bull's-eye of an enemy atomic attack. Leaving her listeners to ponder this grim fact, she went on to matters related more closely to the state's constitutional convention, namely her ideas about multiple-member districting and the direct election of the President by preferential vote. As in Georgia, she distributed sample ballots for a test. Only three years after her 1911 speech suffrage had been adopted in Montana, largely through her own efforts; could that triumph be repeated? Perhaps not then, not today or tomorrow, but surely at no very distant date, she hoped. Her speech was the most memorable of the convention, one observer remarked.

From Montana she flew to New York on Thursday, March 16, on her way to Syracuse, where a series of interviews, dinners, receptions and speeches had been arranged. Since she had always believed that the gospel of peace could not be instilled in children at too early an age, she particularly enjoyed an invitation to talk to the fourth grade class at a local elementary school on Friday. The next day she gave the principal address at the Onondaga County Women's Political Caucus, and for the third time in three weeks she had a testing of the Direct Preferential Ballot. On Monday, March 20, having returned to New York City, she rose at seven to appear on the Today show with Barbara Walters and Frank McGee. And after a week's rest in Georgia she was again airborne on her way to Philadelphia to tape a TV show with Betty Hughes.

Before the two national conventions took place in July 1972, she attended other local meetings of the Women's Political Caucus in the Middle West, and in April she went east again to give a talk in support of Shirley Chisholm in Boston. Around this time a reporter asked her where she really lived—in Montana, Georgia, or California? "I live in an airplane," Jeannette replied. Once in the course of this strenuous tour, when she was spending the night on Long Island at the home of her niece, Mary Elizabeth Huber, Mrs. Huber's husband, a prominent doctor in New York, shook his head gravely when he learned of the schedule Kirkley had planned for Jeannette. Mrs. Huber disagreed with him. Speaking on behalf of the Rankin family, Mary Elizabeth told a visitor that they were not troubled by Jeannette's barnstorming. "She's having a wonderful time," said Mrs. Huber; "she's doing just what she wants to do, and we feel that that is the way she would like to go, right in the midst of things."

The reelection of President Nixon came as no surprise to her; it merely confirmed her in the belief that the Direct Preferential Vote for President should be adopted without delay. The unfolding of the Watergate scandal gave her plan even greater pertinence.

Returning to Georgia somewhat spent, she was obliged to rest for a longer period than she had allowed herself in the frenetic months just past, but her mind was functioning as busily as ever. In her idle moments she plotted schemes whereby women could take nonviolent action against the war in Vietnam, such as abstaining from all shopping on Tuesdays, or refusing to pay the Federal tax on long distance telephone calls. But she knew that these were merely pinpricks, trifling offshoots of her discontent, not drastic enough to satisfy her thirst for action. In reality she hated her idle moments and did everything she could think of to make contact with men and women in public life who were in a position to act boldly. She was tired of talkers, she kept saying; she wanted programs, she wanted someone who would talk back to the government.

One such person was Ralph Nader, whose David-and-Goliath career bore some resemblance to her own. As soon as he sprang into the public eye with his suit against General Motors she had begun writing to him, trying to interest him in her projects, without eliciting any response. In August 1972, however, Nader approached her. He was then engaged in a year-long study of Congress, in the course of which he sent out questionnaires to all former senators and representatives, asking their views on needed congressional reforms. "The most spirited and fundamental response came from Jeannette Rankin," he wrote in his newspaper column for September 14. Not satisfied that her answers to the questionnaire were explicit enough, she flew to Washington to confer with him and his student aides about her plan for multimember districting.

Jeannette referred to her association with Nader as "a love affair." At the time of this latest trip to Washington she was suffering from a slight impediment in her speech; nevertheless she spoke to Nader and his students for some four hours, claiming happily that she had made herself quite clear to them. Nader for his part was struck by her fresh approach to political problems and what he called "the combination of her idealism with a practical sense of citizen responsibility." He saw in her a "future-directed person," tireless in pursuit of her ends. "A forty-hour-a-week job isn't worth doing," she told him. "I'm a bit more frustrated now, however; I worked for suffrage for years, and got it. I've worked for peace for fifty-five years, and haven't come close." Owning up to her age—she was then over ninety-two—she said that she was thinking of running for Congress again, "just to have someone to vote for."

Listening to this intrepid old fighter, Nader was warmed by her ardor and spurred by her unquenchable vitality. "If aging is the erosion of one's ideals," he wrote, "then Jeannette Rankin is young forever." Her session with Nader was, however, her last effort. The speech impediment of which she was conscious at that time was only a symptom of a graver disorder: a degeneration of the muscles of the throat that made swallowing as well as speech difficult, so that in the course of a few months she lost a great deal of weight. It became hard for her to grasp things with her hands, and she was quickly exhausted by even a short walk. At her retirement home she commanded complete medical services, but there was evidently nothing that could be done to reverse the trend.

On the other hand, her mind was as active as ever; she continued to give interviews, keep up her correspondence, and discuss public affairs with her old energy and partisanship, struggling painfully to make herself understood. Mistrusting the doctors' diagnosis, she spoke of plans to go to Mexico to study Spanish, in the expectation that acquiring a new language would be of therapeutic value. On one occasion in those last months she spoke to an old friend about a magazine article concerning World War I which she wanted the friend to read. Believing that she had lent the magazine to someone at the Manor, she made four telephone calls to inquire about it, but no one could understand what she was talking about. As she hung up the receiver, she gave her friend a look of inexpressible woe and burst into tears.

At the Carmel Valley Manor she was surrounded by loving friends and admiring acquaintances; her sister Edna, who lived close by, stood by faithfully, coming once or twice a day to fulfill small commissions. One evening when Jeannette's studio was filled with visitors, one of those present observed how she sat mute through the discussion, only her eyes and half-smile indicating how mindful she was of every remark. The talk turned to the question of euthanasia, or mercy killing, for those whose lives could be prolonged only at the expense of their physical and mental functions. Jeannette was the oldest of the group, and the observer glanced at Jeannette to see if she was pained by the subject. On the contrary; her smile was more pronounced; her eyes lit up; this was an idea with which she was in perfect sympathy.

No such solution proved to be necessary. Though she grew feebler each day, she clung to her interest in the world outside enough to watch the hearings of the Senate Committee on Presidential Elections on television "with glee," as Edna reported, right up to the end. She died in her sleep the night of Friday, May 18, 1973, a few weeks short of her ninety-third birthday.

Acknowledgments and Sources

It was my good fortune to have known Jeannette Rankin over a period of twenty years: I therefore had the opportunity to observe her in her private as well as her public roles. I was her guest in Georgia and in California; and in several informal interviews in which she answered my questions with characteristic forthrightness and candor, I was able to profit by her inimitable comments on the affairs of the day and of the past. It was from this experience that I have drawn the portrait in this book.

Miss Rankin's sister, Edna McKinnon; her niece, Mary Elizabeth Huber; her one-time secretary, Belle Winestine; and her friend, Jeannette Mirsky, have given me significant insights into her personality. I am especially indebted to Mrs. McKinnon and her daughter Dorothy Brown for reading the manuscript and pointing out errors of fact. Among others to whom acknowledgments are due are John Board, John Kirkley, Reita Rivers, Bernice B. Nichols, curator of the Swarthmore College Peace Collection, and Malca Chall and Willa Baum of the Oral History Project of the University of California at Berkeley. My husband's contribution, as always, has been to mingle useful criticism with generous encouragement at every stage.

Bibliography

Unpublished material

Board, John C. *The Lady from Montana: Jeannette Rankin.* Master's Thesis, University of Wyoming, June 1964.

Harris, Ted C. *Jeannette Rankin, Warring Pacifist.* Master's Thesis, University of Georgia, 1969.

Lindquist, Adah Donan. *A Study of Jeannette Rankin and Her Role in the Peace Movement.* Honors Paper, Swarthmore College, December 1971.

Oral History Project, The Bancroft Library, University of California, Berkeley. *Alice Paul Transcript. Jeannette Rankin Transcript.*

Schaffer, Ronald. *Jeannette Rankin, Progressive Isolationist.* Doctoral Dissertation, Princeton University, 1959.

Government Publications

Congressional Record, 65th Congress, 1st Session, May 28, 1917

Hearings before the Committee on Woman Suffrage, House of Representatives, 65th Congress, 2nd Session, January 3–7, 1918

Hearings before the Committee on Foreign Affairs, House of Representatives, 75th Congress, 1st Session, February 16–23, 1937

Hearings before the Committee on Foreign Affairs, House of Representatives, 76th Congress, 1st Session, April 18, 1939

Congressional Record, Volume 87, Part I, 77th Congress, 1st Session, 1941

Congressional Record, Volume 116, Part 15, 91st Congress, 2nd Session, Senate, June 22, 1970

Books

Anthony, Katharine. *Feminism in Germany and Scandinavia.* New York: Henry Holt and Company, 1915.

Bjorkman, Frances M. and Annie G. Porrett, Eds. *Woman Suffrage: History, Arguments, Results.* New York: National Woman Suffrage Publishing Company, 1917.

Burlingame, Merrill G. and K. Ross Toole. *History of Montana.* New York: Lewis Publishing Company, 1957.

Connolly, Christopher P. *The Devil Learns to Vote: The Story of Montana.* New York: Covici Friede, 1938.

Coolidge, Olivia. *Women's Rights, the Suffrage Movement in America, 1848–1920.* New York: Dutton, 1966.

Curti, Merle. *Peace or War, The American Struggle, 1636–1936.* New York: W. W. Norton and Company, 1936.

Day, Dorothy. *The Long Loneliness.* New York: Harper & Bros., 1952.

Degen, Marie Louise. *The History of the Woman's Peace Party.* Baltimore: The Johns Hopkins Press, 1939.

Detzer, Dorothy. *Appointment on the Hill.* New York: Henry Holt, 1948.

Erikson, Erik H. *Gandhi's Truth on the Origins of Militant Nonviolence.* New York: W. W. Norton and Company, 1969.

Flexner, Eleanor. *A Century of Struggle.* Cambridge, Mass.: Harvard University Press, 1959.

Goldmark, Josephine Clara. *Impatient Crusader.* Urbana, Illinois: University of Illinois Press, 1953.

Harper, Ida Husted, Ed. *The History of Woman Suffrage,* Vol. 5–6. New York: National American Woman Suffrage Association, 1922.

Howard, Joseph Kinsey. *Montana, High Wide and Handsome.* New Haven: Yale University Press, 1959.

Hutchens, John K. *One Man from Montana.* Philadelphia: Lippincott, 1964.

Irwin, Inez Haynes. *Angels and Amazons.* Garden City: Doubleday, Doran & Co., 1933.

Kidd, Benjamin. *Social Evolution.* New York: Macmillan Company, 1915.

Libby, Frederick J. *To End War.* Nyack, New York: Fellowship Publications, 1969.

Marx, Karl, and Friedrich Engels. *The Woman Question.* New York: International Publishers, 1951.

Mill, John Stuart. *On Liberty. The Subjection of Women.* New York: H. Holt and Company, 1877.

Miller, Joaquin. *An Illustrated History of the State of Montana.* Chicago: The Lewis Publishing Company, 1894.

Montana, a State Guide Book. American Guide Series, compiled by the Federal Writers' Project. New York: The Viking Press, 1939.

Roosevelt, Eleanor. *My Days.* New York: Dodge Publishing Company, 1938.

Shaw, Anna Howard, with Elizabeth Jordan. *The Story of a Pioneer.* New York: Harper & Bros., 1915.

Slayden, Ellen Maury. *Washington Wife.* New York: Harper & Row, 1962.

Toole, K. Ross. *Montana: An Uncommon Land.* Norman: University of Oklahoma Press, 1959.

Victory: How Women Won It; A Centennial Symposium, by the National Woman Suffrage Association. New York: The H. W. Wilson Company, 1940.

Vorse, Mary Heaton. *Footnote to Folly.* New York: Farrar & Rinehart, 1935.

Wheeler, Burton K., with Paul F. Healy. *Yankee from the West.* Garden City: Doubleday & Company, 1962.

Magazines

American Studies, University of Kansas, Spring 1972. "Peace Movements"

The Classmate, October 1971. "Commitment Knows No Season," by Barbara Saville

Ladies' Home Journal, August 17, 1917. "What We Women Should Do," by Jeannette Rankin

McCall's Magazine, January 1958. "Three Women of Courage," by John F. Kennedy

Montana: The Magazine of Western History, 1967–1973

Montana Historian, Autumn 1972. "Jeannette Rankin, the Lady from Montana," by Phil Rostad

Newsweek, February 14, 1966

Ramparts Magazine, February 1968. "History of the Rise of the Unusual Movement for Women Power in the United States, 1961–68," by W. and M. Hinckle

The Survey, July 21 and 28, 1917

Woman's Home Companion, July–September 1926. "Our Gypsy Journey to Georgia," by Katharine Anthony

Newspapers

Boston Globe, April 7, 1972
Christian Science Monitor, February 14, 1971
The Missoulian, July 7, 1972
New York Times, 1917–19, 1940–42, 1968, 1970, 1971, *passim.*
San Francisco Examiner, June 5, 1970
Washington Post, June 12, 1970
Woman's Journal, 1913–17

Index

Italics indicate pages on which illustrations appear.